New Forest Walks

a time traveller's guide

New Forest Walks

a time traveller's guide

Andrew Walmsley

Published by Sigma Leisure – an imprint of
Sigma Press, Stobart House, Pontyclerc, Penybanc Road
Ammanford, Carmarthenshire SA18 3HP

British Library Cataloguing in Publication Data

A CIP record for this book is available from the British Library

ISBN: 978-1-85058-911-2

Typesetting and Design by: Sigma Press, Ammanford, Carms

Walk route maps and photographs: © Andrew Walmsley

Cover photographs: above: Spring in Brinken Wood; below: Heathland near Hampton Ridge

Printed by: Akcent Media Ltd

Disclaimer: The information in this book is given in good faith and is believed to be correct at the time of publication. Care should always be taken when walking in hill country. Where appropriate, attention has been drawn to matters of safety. The author and publisher cannot take responsibility for any accidents or injury incurred whilst following these walks. Only you can judge your own fitness, competence and experience. Do not rely solely on sketch

Preface

The New Forest has much to attract walkers, for within its bounds are 266 square kilometres (103 square miles) of Crown-owned lands that offer marvellously unrestricted access for people to go largely where they please.

Winter walks on crisp, frosty days are a special delight, whilst spring-like weather sometimes comes as early as February. March brings the spectacular blossoming of the gorse, followed in the woods by the unforgettable April appearance of hazy, fresh green foliage. Misty morns and panoramic landscapes ablaze with heather blossom are a not-to-be-missed feature of late summer, preceding autumnal arboreal displays of gold, red and orange.

But there is far more to the New Forest than wide open spaces and nature's splendour, as these walks well-illustrate; for whilst each includes magnificently varied scenery, all also take visitors past frequently overlooked features deep in the countryside that help reveal the age of this ancient place; features such as upturned pudding basin Bronze Age barrows, Iron Age hillforts, centuries-old charcoal burners' pits, medieval keeper's lodges, mysterious mounds, earthen banks, long forgotten leaf-filled ditches, aged lichen-clad trees that once would have been felled and used for Navy timber, and much, much more.

Each and every one has tales to tell of the prehistoric peoples, Romans, Normans and later men who lived, worked and hunted here; tales that within these pages are brought vividly to life as the New Forest's secret past is revealed. This book does not, though, set out to provide a comprehensive historical account, but simply contributes a sprinkling of information that will greatly enhance the enjoyment of walking in the New Forest.

Sixteen walks are included, with seven shorter versions interspersed amongst the main routes. Spread throughout the area and suitable for all seasons, there is something here for everyone whatever their taste, level of fitness and walking preferences.

- Distances vary from an extremely modest 2 kilometres (1¼ miles) up to 10.5 kilometres (6½ miles)
- Few significant hills will be encountered, and there are virtually no stiles over which to climb
- Some of the walks, as indicated in the text, are suitable for those with young children in buggies
- Public transport users are well-catered for by six walks that start near railway stations, and there are also bus service options. All, though, also

pass through or close to public car parks
- Many of the start points are located around the periphery of the New Forest, which removes the need for motorists to travel into the often busier, more congested centre
- There are countless convenient pub stops along the way, either on or near the walk routes.

Plentiful opportunities are also provided for walkers to create their own routes by combining elements of connecting or nearby walks contained in this book and in the companion volume, New Forest Walks – a seasonal wildlife guide, which is also published by Sigma Press – publication date, November 2012.

And finally, I sincerely hope that readers and walkers find as much of interest within these pages as I found whilst researching and writing the book.

Andrew Walmsley
Melkridge
March 2012

Contents

Introduction

Located close to the south coast in a delightful corner of Hampshire, the New Forest lies between Christchurch to the west and Southampton to the east. The Isle of Wight is a short distance away across The Solent, whilst Salisbury and Winchester, historic cities both, are a little to the north-west and north-east, respectively. Average sunshine hours exceed those experienced in much of Britain, and year-round temperatures are relatively high, with infrequent heavy frost or snow.

The New Forest is not, though, a wholly wooded forest in the modern sense, for this heathland, wetland and woodland landscape was set aside in the late 11th century, during the reign of William the Conqueror, as a Royal Forest, a hunting ground specifically for use by the King and his followers. Forest Law was imposed, and with it came draconian measures designed to protect the deer and the vegetation that sustained them. Punishments were severe for those foolish, or desperate, enough to transgress.

Nor is this place new, for it was known even in William's time as *Nova Foresta*, or the New Forest.

Forest Law was imposed, and with it came draconian measures designed to protect the deer

The New Forest is, however, almost unique in modern Britain, for whilst changes have inevitably occurred – the emphasis on hunting, for example, gradually declined as the importance of timber production increased – continued Crown ownership; jealously guarded common rights; the presence of extensive areas of acidic, relatively infertile soil; and in more recent times, nature conservation interests have all conspired to limit the wholesale transformation that has afflicted much of the wider countryside. Indeed, such is the significance of the New Forest that in 2005 it, together with parts of the surrounding area, was designated a National Park, the first to be created for nearly 50 years.

Here for the visitor, year-round interest is assured in an ever-varied landscape where ancient, unenclosed woodlands abut more recent forestry inclosures; where lowland heaths snuggle quietly beside wildlife-rich valley mires; and clear, swift flowing streams rush ever seawards. Areas of modestly high ground can also be found in the north and west of the area, creating scenery of altogether wilder character than much of that elsewhere.

Commoners' animals roam free. Ponies, donkeys, cattle, autumnal pigs and small numbers of sheep and mules are all part of a centuries-old way of life that used to be widespread over much of Britain, but now elsewhere has largely disappeared, a victim of pressure from the modern world.

The New Forest is not wholly wooded, as can be seen here at Black Bush Plain – Walk 3

Attractive towns and villages – Ashurst, Beaulieu, Brockenhurst, Burley, Downton, Fordingbridge, Lymington, Lyndhurst, Minstead and Ringwood – occur throughout and adjacent to the New Forest, offering accommodation for visitors, pubs, restaurants, a wide range of shops and many other attractions.

Traditional historic interest is also high. Lyndhurst, for example, has the imposing part-17th century Queen's House, the attached Verderers' Hall, and the somewhat extravagant 19th century parish church of St. Michael and All Angels. Beaulieu has Palace House and historic Beaulieu Abbey, recalling 13th century Cistercian presence; whilst nearby Buckler's Hard was the site of a busy 18th century shipbuilding centre.

Wildlife, too, is impressive, both in terms of variety and abundance, and will be fully described in a separate book in this series – *New Forest Walks – a seasonal wildlife guide* – which includes walks that take the visitor to some of the New Forest's more out-of-the-way places where deer can sometimes be seen throughout the day, where myriad birds haunt quiet woodland glades, and scarce wild flowers enrich the scene.

Yes, there is certainly much to enjoy in William's New Forest.

Walking through time

Walking through time! It is a cliché, certainly, but one that can hardly be avoided when considering the New Forest, for here can be found an impressive variety of features that, when considered together, vividly illustrate England's rich heritage. Historical information included with the walks brings to life reminders of the past seen along the way, whilst the broad chronological sequence set out below provides an overall perspective.

Earthen banks and hollows mark the site of the 16th century Saltpetre House near Ashurst

Common rights and commoners' stock

Ancient beech trees adorn the eroded earthen bank of the medieval Park Pale – Walk 8

Walks overview and some advice

Ratings and estimated timings

As a guide, each walk has been allocated a 'degree of difficulty' rating:

1 - Easy walking	Up to 5.5 kilometres (3½ miles), mainly on level ground
2 - Moderate	Between 6 and 9 kilometres (3¾ - 5 ½ miles) with, on some walks, occasional relatively steep uphill sections
3 - Quite strenuous	Over 6 kilometres with some quite steep uphill sections

Estimated times to allow for completion are also provided, although only for general guidance as individual walking speeds will clearly vary. Be sure to use the estimates with care, though, for all the walks are best enjoyed at a slow, relaxed pace with plenty of time set aside to stop, look around and absorb the joys of this most tranquil of places. And always allow enough time to finish the routes in daylight, for finding the way in a darkened wood, for example, can be extremely difficult.

Alternative routes

Seven walks have shorter alternatives available, shown using green arrows on the maps. Many also connect with or pass close to other routes detailed in this book and in New Forest Walks – a seasonal wildlife guide, which provides opportunities to combine elements from multiple routes to create new walks tailored to individual requirements and preferences.

Children's buggies

The suitability of each route for children's buggies is indicated. For this purpose, sturdy, often 3-wheeled, off-road buggies suitable for use in the countryside are assumed, rather than the lighter-weight models designed for pavement use.

Footwear

Always remember that parts of the New Forest, particularly in winter and after rain, can be very wet and muddy, and that even the smallest of streams can temporarily become so swollen that crossing may prove difficult. It is therefore advisable, apart from when using routes that are wholly along gravel tracks, to wear strong, preferably waterproof footwear.

Take care (and an Ordnance Survey map)

Fully numbered directions and correspondingly numbered route maps are provided, but walkers are reminded that there is always a need for care and attention to avoid missing the way – there are no signposts or public footpath signs to help, although cycle tracks are often clearly marked. (Reading ahead is also good advice, as this will help provide an overall context for the walk).

It is also strongly recommended that the Ordnance Survey map of the area - Explorer OL22 - should be carried on the walks, not for use in preference to the provided maps, but as a source of supplementary information. Available at Tourist

Information Centres, bookshops and local newsagents, the Ordnance Survey map will be particularly helpful should walkers stray from the intended route and for walks labelled 'Off the beaten track' - these, at least in part, use minor paths, often through ancient, unenclosed woodlands where one leafy glade can appear much the same as the next, or across heathlands that can appear equally, bafflingly similar.

Please be aware, though, that some paths shown on the Ordnance Survey map are not always visible on the ground, and that those on the ground do not always appear on the map! (This also applies to the presence, or otherwise, of footbridges across streams and drainage channels).

Many of the walks are suitable for families with young children

Also remember that reference may be made in the route directions to aspects of the landscape – the presence of patches of gorse and areas of woodland, for example – that might significantly change following Forestry Commission management programmes involving heathland burning and tree felling; and that summer vegetation – particularly bracken – can obscure paths and tracks that at other times of the year are clearly visible.

Access to a compass, and mobile phone for use in emergencies, might also be helpful, and so might GPS facilities, particularly if combined with a detailed mapping application. Please note, though, that signal coverage in the New Forest cannot always be guaranteed.

Footpath and car park closures

Be aware, also, that the Forestry Commission occasionally temporarily restricts public access to paths and tracks whilst tree thinning or other management work is underway. Similarly, after timber harvesting operations, routes may be closed to allow reinstatement and consolidation following repeated use by heavy vehicles.

In these circumstances, access to an Ordnance Survey map is almost essential as comprehensive diversion signs may not be present.

Additionally, primarily to reduce surface damage, a number of car parks are often closed from early November until late March, so almost all these walks feature at least one alternative start point. A small number of car parks may also be closed in spring to help minimise disturbance to ground nesting birds. Details of closures are available from the Forestry Commission by telephoning 023 80283141 or by checking their web site at **www.forestry.gov.uk/forestry/infd-6g3blb**

Enjoy the walks

Whilst walkers should to be aware of the potential difficulties associated with some New Forest walks, please remember that if the way is occasionally missed or an obstacle is encountered, a willingness to shrug the shoulders and remain relaxed will help ensure continued enjoyment.

Walk maps key:

Red lines with arrows	Route
Red lines without arrows	Paths and tracks not used
Green lines with arrows	Shorter routes
Dark blue lines with arrows	Alternative means of joining the main route (Walk 6 only)
Pink lines with arrows	A detour to additional points of interest (Walk 16 only)
Green background	Woodland
Brown lines	'A' and other roads
Black lines	Inclosure and other boundaries, and the railway
Blue lines	Streams, rivers, ponds, drainage channels
Grey and black lines together	Linear historical features
P	Parking

New Forest Walks - a time traveller's guide

Map of the area

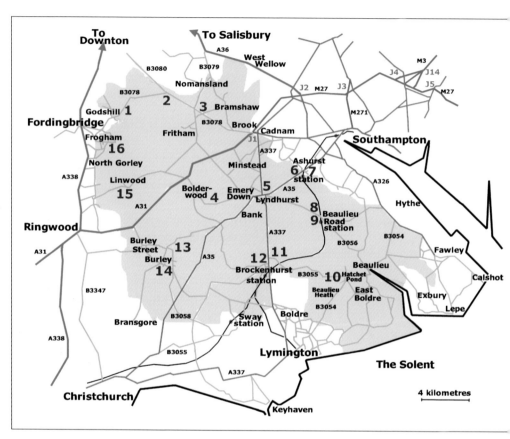

Walk numbers are shown in blue

Map key

Green background	The New Forest
Blue lines	Motorways
Green lines	Primary routes
Red lines	Other 'A' roads
Yellow lines	Minor roads
Black lines	Railway and coastal outline

Public Transport

Train services
The main London Waterloo to Weymouth railway line passes through the New Forest. Stations are at Ashurst (New Forest), Beaulieu Road, Brockenhurst and Sway. For details of the service, telephone National Rail Enquiries on 08457 484950 or visit **www.nationalrail.co.uk**

Bus services
Bluestar buses operate from Southampton to Lymington, passing along the A35 between Ashurst and Lyndhurst; and along the A337 between Lyndhurst, Brockenhurst and Lymington. Further details are available by telephoning 023 80231950 or visiting **www.bluestarbus.co.uk**

Wilts and Dorset buses operate from Lymington to Hythe, via Beaulieu; from Christchurch to Ringwood via Burley; and from Bournemouth to Salisbury, via Fordingbridge. Further details are available by telephoning 01983 827005 or visiting **www.wdbus.co.uk**

National Express operates a service between London and Bournemouth. It stops once per day in each direction – at Brockenhurst and Lyndhurst. For further details, telephone 08717 818181 or check the web site – **www.nationalexpress.com/coach**

Consider, too, using a New Forest Tour Bus – they typically operate from late June to mid-September along circular routes following: a) the A337 between Lymington, Brockenhurst and Lyndhurst; the B3056 between Lyndhurst and Beaulieu, with a detour to Exbury; and the B3054 from Beaulieu back to Lymington, and b) between Ashurst, Lyndhurst, Burley, Ringwood, Fordingbridge, Brook, Cadnam and Woodlands. The buses can be flagged down along the way and will stop whenever it is safe to do so. For further information and to confirm service dates, ring 0871 2002233 or check out **www.thenewforesttour.info/**

As services are regularly reviewed and revised, visitors are advised to contact the relevant operator before travelling.

Additional information
The Public Transport Traveline on 0871 2002233 can provide additional information about local public transport facilities, or refer to **www.traveline.org.uk/index.htm**

Some dos and don'ts

Apologies are probably due here to the great majority of New Forest walkers, as many of the following dos and don'ts will be completely obvious to many people. But for the absolute avoidance of doubt, please treat this wonderful place with the greatest of respect and in particular:

Do not damage the archaeology or other historic features
* Do not be tempted to undertake archaeological or other digs without first consulting the New Forest National Park Authority
* Do not damage ancient New Forest earthworks or other historic features
* Never take away items of any kind from historic sites.

Help safeguard New Forest wildlife
* From March to July, a range of scarce, vulnerable heathland and wetland birds nest on or close to the ground. To avoid causing disturbance, stay on the main paths at this time, and ensure that dogs do not stray from the paths
* If you find a new-born deer, leave it alone as mum will probably not be far away
* Avoid close contact with reptiles. All are harmless to people, apart, that is, from adders, that can inflict a nasty, poisonous but rarely fatal bite. Even they, though, much prefer to quietly retreat in the face of potential danger, but will respond aggressively if suddenly disturbed or if attempts are made to handle them. Good advice, then, is to leave them well alone, and reduce the likelihood

Never pick or uproot wild flowers such as this heath spotted orchid

of a chance encounter by staying on heathland paths where reptiles are likely to be clearly visible

- Do not be tempted to pick wild flowers or uproot plants – this potentially damages the ecology of the New Forest, harms the individual species concerned, and is often illegal
- Observe the New Forest Fungi Code: there is a 1.5 kg (3¹/₃ lbs) personal collecting limit, commercial collecting is not allowed, never remove all the fungi present in an area, obey all related warning signs, and take great care with identification – some species are extremely poisonous and may even be fatal if eaten.

Take all litter home

- Litter is unsightly and, if trodden on or eaten, can have unfortunate consequences for wild animals and commoners' stock.

Remember that the commoners' animals are not pets

- Ponies and other stock animals are largely harmless, although some are not averse to nipping or kicking those who get too close. Good advice is to always keep a sensible distance away from them
- Do not feed the animals. It is bad for their diet, attracts them to roadsides and car parks where traffic accidents may occur, and encourages nuisance begging
- Unless instructed otherwise, close gates behind you. (To encourage the development of conditions where wild flowers and insects flourish, commoners' animals are deliberately excluded from many of the woodland inclosures. Open gates are an invitation that few animals can resist. Ponies are, however, permitted to enter a small number of inclosures where gates are locked open)
- Avoid the annual pony drifts, the late summer and autumnal animal round-ups. Casual watchers, however well-intentioned, are likely to get in the way of this serious element of commoning life
- And motorists, please be aware of the idiosyncrasies of the animals. They often frequent roadsides, but have developed little sense of the dangers associated with cars and other vehicles. Consequently, many are victims of road traffic accidents, so please be careful when driving, always keep within the speed limits, and appreciate that animal behaviour can at times be unpredictable.

Start	Ashley Walk, Forestry Commission car park 1.25 kilometres (¾ mile) north-east of Godshill on the B3078 Brook to Fordingbridge road - Ordnance Survey map reference SU186156
Distance	10.5 kilometres (6½ miles) Shorter walk: 9 kilometres (5½ miles)
Time to allow	2½ - 6½ hours
Refreshments	The Fighting Cocks, Godshill, is close to the start of the walk
Route	Along readily visible tracks
Terrain	Mainly on level ground, but with a small number of quite steep, uphill sections. Note, however, that in winter and after heavy rain, the stream through Pitts Wood Inclosure can become badly swollen, and may require a detour to left or right to find a suitable crossing place
Rating	3 - in places, quite strenuous walking
Buggies	Except after rain, the route in late spring and summer is usually suitable for sturdy buggies, although a couple of short stretches in Pitts Wood Inclosure can be a little awkward to negotiate, and the ground can be a little wet in other places
Railway station	Ashurst (New Forest), 19 kilometres (12 miles)
Bus service	Wilts and Dorset serve nearby Fordingbridge
New Forest Tour Bus	Yes
Alternative starts	1) Deadman Hill, Forestry Commission car park at Ordnance Survey map reference SU192165 2) Godshill Cricket, Forestry Commission car park at Ordnance Survey map reference SU182151
Forest Holidays Caravan sites and campsites	1) Longbeech, 10 kilometres (6¼ miles) 2) Ocknell, 11 kilometres (7 miles)

Walk 1
Ashley Walk Bombing Range, Cockley Hill, Leaden Hall, The Butts, Coopers Hill and Pitts Wood Inclosure

Ponies on Hampton Ridge

Setting the scene

Located on relatively high ground in the north of the New Forest, the site of the Second World War, Ashley Walk Bombing Range might seem an unusual choice for a stroll, but peace and tranquility returned long ago to this timeless landscape of extensive heathlands, broad valleys and mixed-age woodland.

Along the way, Bronze Age barrows and a Roman road keep silent company with oft-forgotten reminders of the range; whilst an ancient ridge-way route provides distant views towards Wiltshire and Dorset amidst rugged scenery that contrasts sharply with the often gentler terrain found in the southern parts of the New Forest.

Along the way

Ashley Walk - the bombing range

Desperate times call for desperate measures, and few times have been more desperate for Britain than the Second World War years. Rising to the challenge, the

New Forest responded with vigour to the national need. Airfields were constructed where before had been open heathland; an extensive armaments research establishment was created; 'Special Forces' trained undercover; troops and equipment were assembled on the open Forest, waiting to be called into overseas action; anti-aircraft guns peppered the night sky; and common land was ploughed and used for food production.

Here in the north of the New Forest, in mid-1940 a bombing range was also established. Centred on Ashley Cross, a little to the south of Ashley Bottom, it covered more than 2,025 hectares (5,000 acres), was enclosed by 14.5 kilometres (9 miles) of fencing, and included a high explosive range and a considerably smaller practice range, part of which is visited during Walk 16.

Mosquitos, Lancaster bombers, Flying Fortresses and a range of other aircraft and equipment were used to test weaponry, bombs, bombing techniques and

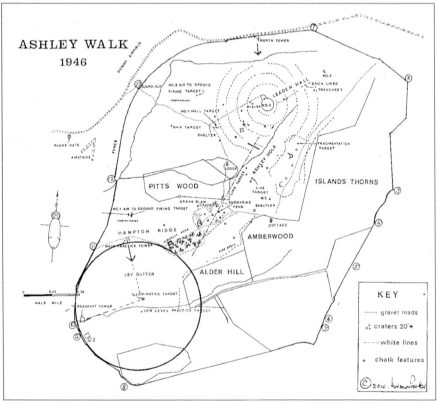

A sketch map showing the Ashley Walk bombing range and many of its features
(courtesy of Norman Parker)

Bomb craters remain conspicuously present

methods of delivery. Bomb craters, in places, remain conspicuously present. Wartime's heaviest bomb, the 10,000 kg (22,000 lbs) 'Grand Slam', for example, left a crater 40 metres (130 feet) across and over 21 metres (70 feet) deep, although now only an in-filled, marshy depression can be seen quite close to the southern boundary of Pitts Wood Inclosure.

Control and observation towers were built, and observation huts, too. Servicemen were billeted on the lawn opposite a local inn - The Fighting Cocks at Godshill - close to two airstrips constructed for use by light aircraft.

The range closed in 1946 and the surrounding fence was removed in 1948.

Wall targets

A number of targets were constructed on the range, including two enormous sets of parallel, reinforced concrete walls, the No. 1 and 2 Wall Targets, both 12 metres (40 feet) high by 12 metres wide. A third wall, the No. 3 Wall Target, provided test facilities for the 'Bouncing Bombs' of Dr. Barnes Wallis, and was 6 metres (20 feet) wide - later extended to 27 metres (90 feet) - 2.7 metres (9 feet) high and 1.8 metres (6 feet) thick, faced with 5 centimetre (2 inch) armour plating. Filled with inert material rather than explosives, the bombs used against

Commoners' stock on the site of the No.2 Wall Target

these targets tested casing strength and initiating systems.

The walls were demolished shortly after the range closed, although the concrete aprons of the No. 1 and 2 targets remained until 1991 when they were broken up, crushed and reused for road construction. The No. 3 target, so it is said, was simply toppled into a trench and buried, leaving just a long mound as evidence of its presence.

Ministry of Home Security Target

Originally known as the Ministry of Home Security Target, and later, but incorrectly, as the Submarine Pens, a huge concrete structure a little to the south of Pitts Wood Inclosure was until recently believed to have simulated facilities used along the French coast to protect German submarines. Updated information, however, provided by Norman Parker, writer and authority on the bombing range, confirms that it was simply an above-ground, reinforced concrete shell used to test response to bombs, some of which were exploded from within. The structure, though, resisted substantial damage and when no longer needed proved impractical to remove. It was eventually buried and now appears as a large, vegetation-topped mound with concrete pushing through where erosion has removed the covering of earth.

The Ministry of Home Security Target appears now as a large, vegetation-topped mound.

Section of the line target

Line target and Ship target

Terminated by a large cross, a 'line target' 3 metres (10 feet) wide and 1,829 metres (6,000 feet) long was marked out with imported chalk to simulate an enemy railway line; whilst a 'ship target', made from 1.25 cm (½") thick steel plates, represented part of a merchant ship's hull that was used to test a variety of air-to-ground rockets.

Little of substance remains of the 'ship target' apart from a concrete base with protruding metal bolts; but the 'line target' is still clearly visible in places, and during this walk is best seen adjacent to the Ministry of Home Security Target where to the south-west its course now forms a pronounced track through the gorse.

Fragmentation bomb targets

Close to the Ministry of Home Security Target, the outline of a large, chalk letter 'B' continues to mark one of the areas used to test fragmentation bombs designed to explode when 6 – 9 metres (20 – 30 feet) above the ground, creating a substantial 'blast' effect and showering bomb splinters on personnel and equipment below.

Still clearly visible, the letter 'B' marked out in chalk

Here, and in the adjacent 'A' area a little to the south-west, dispersal pens containing unwanted aircraft were set in place to test the pens' protection characteristics, although little evidence now remains except for traces of earthwork enclosures. (The unwanted aircraft included new, U.S. built P-39 Airacobra fighters that on at least one occasion, when senior U.S. officers were present on the range, were hidden to avoid causing offence).

Separately, at Coopers Hill, in range areas 'C' and 'D', fragmentation bomb trials targeted trenches containing wooden dummies placed to simulate troops.

Amberwood Cottage and Ashley Lodge - remote dwellings lost to the bombing

Use of the area as a bombing range displaced the residents of two dwellings that, sadly, were described in a contemporary Manual of Armament Testing as *Miscellaneous Targets.*

Amberwood Cottage, built in around 1815, stood on the northern edge of Amberwood Inclosure, close to Ashley Cross. It was badly damaged by the bombing and subsequently demolished, although the stable block foundations and some garden trees – yews and laurels - can still be seen close to the main track leading alongside the inclosure.

Ashley Lodge, located to the north of Pitts Wood Inclosure, dated back to 1773, when an even older structure was rebuilt, but it, too, was so badly damaged during bombing operations that it was demolished after the war. Today, evidence of former occupation

Earth-covered bricks close to the site of Ashley Lodge

includes an earth-covered pile of bricks; brambles, grassland and a mixture of trees that are somewhat out-of-keeping with the wild Forest; old, eroded boundary banks; remnants of the keeper's meadow; and the name of nearby Lodge Hill.

Roman roads – straight and true

Following the Roman invasion of AD 43, much of Britain remained part of the Roman Empire until the early 5th century. In Hampshire, impressive evidence of this period can be found at Silchester and Rockbourne (town and villa sites, respectively), whilst Ackling Dyke, a particularly well-preserved Roman road, passes quite close to the edge of the New Forest on its way from Old Sarum, on the outskirts of Salisbury, to Badbury Rings in Dorset.

A minor track intersects a section of the Roman road

Significant Roman presence in the New Forest is less readily demonstrated, however, although Roman influence certainly left its mark. Remains of Romano-British potteries, for example, lie shrouded in some of the woodlands visited during a number of these walks, a suspected Roman estate boundary is crossed during Walk 10, and the likely line of a Roman road is passed during Walk 7.

Here on the old bombing range, a section of Roman road also survives, its course followed by a later parish boundary. Running on a predictably straight line between Pitts Wood Inclosure and a point close to the site of Amberwood Cottage, the raised agger – the cambered embankment that carried the road – is still visible as a modest, flat-topped mound 4.5-6 metres (15 -20 feet) across. On the heath, it is largely concealed beneath grass, heather, bracken and gorse, and can best be found where a minor track crosses the bump of the agger in the copse shown on the sketch map.

This road ran eastwards to Fritham where another Roman road was met; whilst to the west, the route has not been identified beyond Fordingbridge.

Pitts Wood Inclosure and the first (1698) Act of Parliament to authorise creation of timber plantations

First set aside for trees in the second half of the 18th century, the name of this inclosure recalls John Pitt, Surveyor General of Woods and Forests at the time. An iron plate passed during the walk provides an outline of inclosure history. Put in

Pitts Wood Inclosure

place by Gerald Lascelles, Deputy Surveyor of the New Forest from 1880 to 1914, it reads: 'E R, Pitt's Wood, Enclosed 1775, Thrown out 1816, Re-enclosed 1903.' Today, some oaks from the original and later plantings remain, along with a great many conifers.

But there is more than this to the Pitts Wood Inclosure story, for here is one of the New Forest's earliest Statutory Inclosures, created using the provisions of the 1698 Act for the Increase and Preservation of Timber in the New Forest, the first Act to authorise the creation of plantations following concerns about potential shortages of large timber suitable for Royal Navy shipbuilding.

Previous bad practices, too, were addressed by the Act, although with varying degrees of success. Pollarding of timber trees, for example, was forbidden, and restrictions were placed on charcoal burners, many of whom were suspected of torching large quantities of valuable timber.

But why was an Act of Parliament needed? Well, natural re-generation could not be relied upon to replace trees cut down or otherwise lost; for deer and commoners' stock prevented significant re-growth. Effective management was, then, essential, but the erection of fencing to keep out the animals was forbidden – commoners' rights to put out stock were to be recognised and respected, and the deer were still to have freedom to roam. The solution: an Act of Parliament that specifically authorised enclosure.

Other Acts authorising the further creation of inclosures followed, too: in 1808 (details are included with Walk 6), 1851 (see Walk 9) and, to a lesser extent, in 1949. All were to have a dramatic impact on the New Forest landscape as heaths, lawns, scattered hollies and ancient woodlands were lost to timber plantations.

Hive Garn Bottom – peace, quiet, bees and blossom

Hive Garn Bottom borders the northern edge of Pitts Wood Inclosure. Here, persistently damp slopes run down into the valley where mature oaks and ancient hollies have a hold on the dryer, more fertile ground. Gorse adds bold splashes of colour, whilst heather provides a seasonal feast for bees and other insects.

In fact, 'hive' and 'garn' (a contraction of garden) place names, along with 'garden' in full, and 'bee' names, suggest past use by beekeepers who would leave out their hives for the summer months to encourage the residents to forage

Hive Garn Bottom

amongst the blooms – the honey produced is distinctively dark, has a delightful fragrance and is absolutely delicious.

In many of these places, and elsewhere on the heaths, evidence remains of old, small embanked enclosures that are thought to have been used to protect the hives from damage by deer and commoners' stock. Age is often uncertain, although Hive Garn Bottom is so named on Richardson, King and Driver's late 18th century map of the New Forest.

The Route

1. Leave the car park, situated in an old gravel pit beside the appropriately named Gravel Pit Hill, and follow the Snake Road, the original access track to Ashley Lodge, past the site of a bombing range access gate and the guard hut.

   In the valley bottom, cross the Ditchend Brook, a stream that often is dry in summer and early autumn.

   Away to the left here are the remains of the stone quarry that gave this part of the valley its name: Stone Quarry Bottom.

   Follow the track up Cockley Hill beside on the left the heavily browsed, multiple-stemmed hollies of Cockley Bushes; and past at the top, again on the left, a shallow pit.

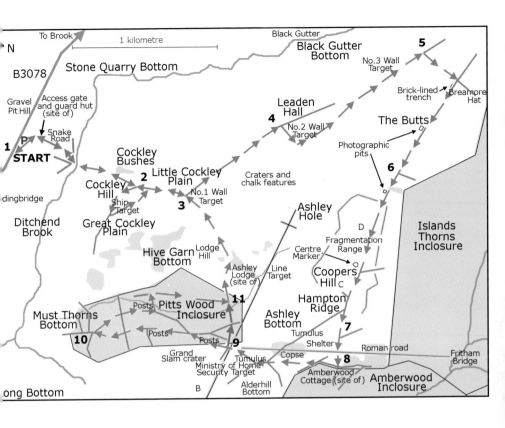

2. A short detour to the right here, heading towards the far end of the ridge, will reveal amongst scattered gorse bushes the remains of the Ship Target. Return to the main walk route by turning left along a gravel track just beyond the concrete. Continue along the main track until a left turn is reached.

   Immediately to the right here are the solidified chalk remains of material originally used to mark out targets and other range features. The site of an observation shelter overlooking the No. 1 Wall Target is adjacent, beside the track leading straight ahead. Bumps, undulations, and occasional pieces of brick and concrete, hint at past usage.

3. Take the left turn. *Almost immediately to the right, at 90 degrees to the track, notice the site of the No. 1 Wall Target, now just a long, shallow, gravel-strewn depression with pieces of masonry and concrete nearby.*

   Continue along this track.

Pass two large craters away to the right, both with prominent surrounding, gravel-capped banks and equally noticeable encroaching willows. A little to the south of that furthest away, out of sight of the main track, is a quite large, pale circular area with interior cross; and nearby, the outline of another large cross pockmarked with bomb craters.

Further along, again to the right, but quite near the track, is a close-cropped area of grass with rectangular mound in its midst, presumably the site of the filming shelter that once overlooked the No. 2 Wall Target.

4. Shortly after, turn right along the edge of a large, open area of grassland, the site of the No. 2 Wall Target.

    When close to the far end of the grassland, go left across a patch of bare earth, before following a quite wide track through the surrounding heather. (In winter and after rain, the bare earth is often muddy, and can be avoided by continuing around the edge of the open area).

    On the left, quite a way along here, running at 90 degrees to the track, is a quite wide earthen bank topped with stunted hawthorns, hollies and a crab apple tree – the site of the No. 3 Wall Target.

5. Turn right immediately before a patch of gorse and hollies, and then right again at a crossroads close to Breamore Hat, a small but attractive oak and holly copse.

    Notice beside the track on the right, 30 metres (100 feet), or so, along here, a line of bricks just visible through the surface soil and running parallel to the track. Around 5 metres (16½ feet) long and 0.5 metres (1½ feet) wide, these are the remains of a brick-lined trench used to shelter servicemen observing and filming the bomb tests.

    Continue straight ahead along Hampton Ridge, past the Bronze Age barrows known as The Butts.

    There are probably six separate barrows, although erosion, past excavation and war-time activity has made a precise count difficult. The first, sadly, has been so badly damaged that walk-in access is possible. Immediately beyond the last barrow, to the right of the path, is a quite large, rectangular shaped depression that is now often filled with water – this is the site of an open pit used for shelter whilst the bomb tests were being filmed.

6. Ignore a pronounced track on the left; and eventually go through the edge of a group of hollies, gorse and oaks.

    Pass on the right another rectangular, often water-filled depression – the site of another photographic pit.

Follow the main track as it intersects a heather, gorse and bracken-topped earthen bank.

The earthen bank – particularly visible on the left – enclosed the 'C' and 'D' areas of the fragmentation bomb test range, and here, to the right of the track, out on the heath, can still be found the pale outline of the letter 'D', its position marked by encroaching hawthorns. The letter 'C' is further on, close to a patch of gorse and a single birch tree.

Pass on the right a short distance from the track, within an area of bare ground, a large chalk circle.

Clearly visible from over-flying aircraft, this indicated the centre of the High Explosive Range. It was used to help pilots and crew obtain a bearing.

And then pass a quite wide track on the left.

7. Continue straight ahead, ignoring minor tracks to right and left.

On the right here is what at first glance appears to be an open-backed, brick-built bus shelter. Viewing slits set in concrete surrounds do, though, offer a clue to its original purpose as an observation shelter associated with the fragmentation range. The end walls display a quite large 'V', presumably anticipating Victory, picked out with contrasting, darker coloured bricks that have mellowed with time.

Further to the right here is a low, bracken covered mound, the remains of another Bronze Age barrow. John Wise told that a labouring man in the 1820s or 1830s opened a barrow near here - maybe it was this one – as he 'constantly dreamt that he should there find a crock of gold.' For his trouble, though, he found only charcoal.

8. Turn right onto a gravel cycle track alongside Amberwood Inclosure and the site of Amberwood Cottage. Follow the cycle track out onto the heath, and eventually consider a short detour to the left to enjoy fine views over Alderhill Bottom.

Go straight ahead at a junction of minor tracks – the course of the Roman road can best be seen to the right here – and immediately after, leave the cycle track by taking the right fork at a 'Y' junction to continue along an equally wide gravel track.

To the left here is yet another Bronze Age barrow that, like the others, somehow survived the bombing; whilst further to the left is a relatively large, gorse and bracken-clad mound upon which grow a number of stunted trees – this is the site of the Ministry of Home Security Target. Nearby is a prominent section of the line target, and the fragmentation bomb test range, 'B' area. Also notice here, to the left of the track, a series of eroded earthen banks that are possibly the remains of war-time trenches.

Ignore minor paths on the right as the main gravel track bears left, downhill; and after a short distance, reach a crossroads.

9. **To take the shorter walk that misses out much of Pitts Wood Inclosure, turn right here, go downhill through the edge of the wood, cross a usually narrow stream and rejoin the main route at the start of Section 11.**
   The iron plate outlining the history of the inclosure can be found as the wood is entered, whilst on either side of the track just before the stream are the ground level remains of structures presumably left over from the bombing range.
   Otherwise, go straight ahead at the crossroads, still downhill; and enter the inclosure between two solid old gateposts. Pass a minor path on the right, immediately take the left fork at a prominent Y-junction, and pass three more substantial posts. Ignore a path going left, uphill, immediately after the posts; continue downhill and then go straight ahead at a crossroads.

10. Turn sharp right at the next crossroads, just before the edge of the wood is reached – a short detour straight ahead here gives good views over Long Bottom and makes a well-sheltered refreshment stop.
    Go straight ahead at another crossroads, and shortly after, pass through a grove of aged hollies and oaks, some of which almost certainly pre-date the original inclosure planting.
    Pass between two more sturdy gateposts; immediately after, turn left at a T-junction; continue downhill along a gravel track, and cross a usually narrow stream.
    The damp, valley-bottom grassland away to the right here is the site of an old meadow associated with Ashley Lodge – it was shown on Richardson, King and Driver's map simply as Meadow.
    Ignore a minor track on the left, and follow the gravel track as it bends round to the right.

11. Turn left at the next T-junction of gravel tracks and continue uphill, eventually past the site of Ashley Lodge.
    On the right along here is a small area of grassland bordered by tangles of trees and brambles, part of the old lodge grounds that today provide an oasis for wildlife. A more extensive area of grassland follows on the left, with, close to the track, building material and a small section of floor recalling former use. To the right of the track here is a low, soil-covered, tree-clad mound of brick rubble and other building material left over from the lodge.
    Pass through a straggle of hollies, and reach open ground close to the top of the hill.

To the right here are views back towards Ashley Hole, whilst a little further on, at the top of the hill, are two bomb craters on the left, the largest of which supports growths of hawthorn, willow and gorse. Beyond, again on the left, are views across Hive Garn Bottom.

At Little Cockley Plain, pass the right turn used on the outward route, and continue straight ahead to return to the car park.

For the adventurous, for those with a good sense of direction, strong map reading skills and access to an Ordnance Survey map!

Create your own walk by combining parts of this route with elements of your choice from the following selection of connecting or conveniently located nearby routes.

From *New Forest Walks - a time traveller's guide:*
Walk 2   Bramshaw Telegraph
Walk 16   Frogham

From *New Forest Walks - a seasonal wildlife guide:*
Walk 1   Godshill Cricket
Walk 2   Ashley Walk, Millersford Bottom

Start	Telegraph Hill, Forestry Commission car park, 5.25 kilometres (3¼ miles) north-west of Brook on the B3078 Fordingbridge road - Ordnance Survey map reference SU228166
Distance	9.5 kilometres (6 miles)
Time to allow	2½ - 6 hours
Refreshments	The Royal Oak, Fritham, is midway through the walk
Route	Largely along readily visible tracks, although a little 'off the beaten track' through Eyeworth Wood
Terrain	Mainly on level ground, but with a small number of quite steep, uphill sections
Rating	3 - in places, quite strenuous walking
Buggies	Except after rain, the route in late spring and summer is usually suitable for sturdy buggies, although the ground in places is quite rutted until Eyeworth Pond is reached, and can be a little wet in other places
Railway station	Ashurst (New Forest), 14 kilometres (8½ miles)
Bus service	None
New Forest Tour Bus	Yes
Alternative starts	1) Eyeworth Pond, Forestry Commission car park, on the route at Ordnance Survey map reference SU228146 2) Fritham, Forestry Commission car park, also on the route, at Ordnance Survey map reference SU231141
Forest Holidays Caravan sites and campsites	1) Longbeech 5.25 kilometres (3¼ miles) 2) Ocknell 6.25 kilometres (4 miles)

Walk 2
Bramshaw Telegraph, Homy Ridge, Eyeworth Wood, Eyeworth Pond, Islands Thorns Inclosure, Coopers Hill and The Butts

Setting the scene

Bramshaw Telegraph, the site of a 19th century signal station, lies beside the B3078 Brook to Fordingbridge road. To the south-east, the walk route crosses a shallow heathland valley before continuing along Homy Ridge, and later takes in the wide open spaces of Hampton Ridge.

Eyeworth Pond

Eyeworth Wood, one of the most impressive of the New Forest's ancient, unenclosed woodlands, is visited; whilst Amberwood and Islands Thorns Inclosures, created in 1815 and 1852, respectively, provide elements of contrast. Eyeworth Pond, bordered in part by trees, is a favourite haunt of geese and ducks that provide further welcome variety.

Along the way

Bramshaw Telegraph - a revolutionary 19th century communication system

At 128 metres (420 feet) above sea level, Bramshaw Telegraph is one of the highest points in the New Forest. It was also the site of a 19th century optical shutter signal station, one in a line that linked Plymouth with the Admiralty in London.

Using a system devised by Lord George Murray, signals were sent by opening and closing six shutters in a vertical frame. Powerful fixed telescopes trained on adjacent stations in the line were used to read the

The Telegraph Hill car park, with Hope Cottage just across the road, is close to the site of Bramshaw Telegraph

signals, which were then relayed on. Transmission speeds were impressive – London messages took about twenty minutes to reach Plymouth.

Manned by a naval officer and two ratings, the wooden building that housed the system is thought to have been located close to Hope Cottage. Adjoining stations were to the north of Verwood, in neighbouring Dorset, and at Toot Hill, near Romsey. The line operated from 1806 until 1847, and was used primarily during the Napoleonic Wars. A similar system was used between London and Portsmouth.

Eyeworth Wood - an ancient, unenclosed woodland

Here in this ancient, unenclosed woodland, all is usually quiet except for the murmur of bird song and the sound of breeze passing through the upper branches of wizened oak and beech trees. Aged sentinels clad in ivy, moss and lichens are haphazardly spaced as decreed by nature, not man. But some have fallen, defeated by winter gales, their knarled old limbs littering the woodland floor where, in the depths of decay, they provide nourishment for a bewildering

A pony grazing in Eyeworth Wood

array of fungi and for stag beetle larvae that will eventually metamorphisise into pugnacious adults.

For centuries, the character of these woods has been shaped by deer and commoners' stock that have created noticeable browse lines, and have removed much of the under-storey vegetation.

Man, too, was quick to use the timber. Charcoal burners plied their trade in these places, often illicitly after the 1698 Act of Parliament imposed restrictions; whilst before the same Act forbade the practice, many oak and beech trees were periodically pollarded, and the re-growth used to feed the deer or for firewood. (Look out, then, in these old woods for multiple-stemmed, mature pollard trees, for it is likely that they pre-date 1698).

Whole trees, too, were taken and the larger timbers used for Navy shipbuilding, so-much-so that potential shortages led to the restrictions already mentioned and the progressive creation of timber growing inclosures.

Statutory protection was provided by the 1877 New Forest Act, yet here in Eyeworth Wood, in Bramshaw Wood and in a number of places elsewhere, old posts betray the past presence of fenced plots created by the Forestry Commission in the 1960s, ostensibly to encourage broadleaved regeneration, but somewhat controversially cleared of many fine, mature trees. Needless to say, the public outcry concerning this and other practices was considerable, and sufficient to eventually halt the destruction.

Eyeworth Pond – a landscape gem with a secret past

Eyeworth Pond is an idyllic beauty spot. Almost completely surrounded by trees, water lilies add a splash of spring and summer colour to the pond, ponies drink at the water's edge, Canada geese are present all-year-round and extravagantly plumaged mandarin ducks feed almost from the hand.

But whilst the pond has all the appearance of a natural feature, the raised bank at the south-western end provides a clue to its origin, for it is, in fact, man-made. Created by damming a small stream in the second half of the 19th century, it was used as a reservoir to hold an estimated 6 million gallons of water needed by the nearby Schultze Gunpowder Factory.

Permission for the project was first given in 1871, but work was delayed following refusal by the company to accept conditions imposed on the development, and objections by the commoners. A new application was eventually made in 1883; Gerald Lascelles, newly appointed Deputy Surveyor of the New Forest, considered that the scheme would add to the beauty of the Forest; and work finally proceeded.

Mandarin ducks on Eyeworth Pond

And Lascelles was, of course, absolutely right, for the pond remains as an impressive landscape feature and wildlife habitat, popular with local residents and visitors alike.

Schultze Gunpowder Factory - once an important local employer

Quiet and tranquil are words often used to describe the New Forest, yet somewhat incongruously, from the mid-19th century until the early years of the 20th century, the Schultze Gunpowder Company, attracted by the remote location, had a large factory in the grounds of Eyeworth Lodge.

Construction started in around 1860, although Captain Schultze, who lent his name to the enterprise, did not become involved until nine years later. Upwards of one hundred people were subsequently employed in sixty buildings.

Little evidence of the factory survives, although the superintend-ent's and gatekeeper's houses remain, and so does an associated track known as the Powder Mill Road. Leading from Eyeworth Pond to the B3078, use of this track avoided the need for the potentially deadly products to travel through Fritham village.

The Schultze Gunpowder Factory post box at Fritham

Look out, too, for an old black, metal post box once associated with the factory, placed to make the postman's life easier in the days before motor vans – it is on the walk route beside the car park entrance at the top of the hill leading down to the pond.

When first approaching Islands Thorns Inclosure, close to the start of Section 7 of the walk, notice also towards the centre of the adjacent field – on the right of the track – a dilapidated magazine once used to store the finished powder. (Even from the track, a brick-built wall with two low, entrance chambers can be seen on the left-hand edge of this quite large, grassy, man-made hillock, riddled now with rabbit burrows.)

Studley Castle - medieval earthworks deep in the woods

The site of Studley Castle, a 14th century keeper's lodge, is now within the much later planting of Islands Thorns Inclosure. A wasted earthen bank still surrounds a rectangular plot of land, and a modest internal ditch also survives. A scatter of West Country slate – the remains of imported roofing material - was found here in 1968. Other medieval New Forest lodges include those located in what is now Churchplace Inclosure, visited during Walk 7; and at Queen Bower, visited during Walk 12.

Wasted earthwork remains of Studley Castle

The Route

1. Follow the path leading half-to-the-left away from the car park, across a varied landscape of heather, gorse, holly, birch and pine; and eventually go downhill into Claypits Bottom.

2. Cross a well-vegetated stream/drainage channel that can be stepped over at most times of year, although there is a bridge a short distance away to the right; and continue uphill towards a quite large, somewhat foreboding holly, pine and oak wood straddling Homy Ridge.

   The wood is called Dark Hat Wood, whilst it has been suggested that Homy is a misspelling of Holmy, a reference to the hollies.

3. On the edge of the wood, turn right along the ridge from where there are good views towards the extensive broadleaved woodlands of Studley Wood, Islands Thorns Inclosure and Eyeworth Wood. Ignore minor tracks to left and right - pathways made by ponies and deer – and eventually follow the main track as it meanders into the peaceful confines of Eyeworth Wood.

4. Pass a grassy track on the right and follow the wider, well-worn, rutted main track as it bears left beside a huge 1960s gatepost. After a short distance, pass on the left an area of relatively recently pollarded hollies, now vigorously regenerating; then further on, pass another old gatepost before continuing gradually downhill.

5. Pass a short distance away on the right, fields associated with Eyeworth Lodge; go beside a low, Forestry Commission vehicle barrier adjacent to the entrance to Oak Tree Cottage; and follow the now gravelled track across a bridge over a tributary of the Latchmore Brook.

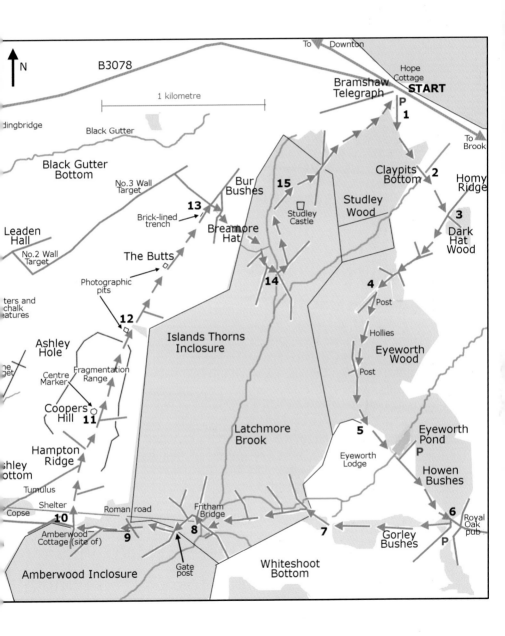

N

B3078

To Downton

Bramshaw
Telegraph

Hope
Cottage

START

P
1

To
Brook

1 kilometre

dingbridge

Black Gutter

Black Gutter
Bottom

Claypits
Bottom

2

Homy
Ridge

No.3 Wall
Target

Bur
Bushes

15

Studley
Wood

13

Studley
Castle

3

Brick-lined
trench

Breamore
Hat

Dark
Hat
Wood

Leaden
Hall

No.2 Wall
Target

The Butts

14

4

Post

Photographic
pits

Hollies

ters and
chalk
atures

12

Eyeworth
Wood

Islands Thorns
Inclosure

Post

Ashley
Hole

ne
get

Centre
Marker

Fragmentation
Range

Coopers
Hill

11

Eyeworth
Pond

P

Latchmore
Brook

5

Hampton
Ridge

Eyeworth
Lodge

Howen
Bushes

shley
ottom

Tumulus

Copse

Shelter

Roman road

Fritham
Bridge

6

Royal
Oak
pub

10

8

7

Amberwood
Cottage (site of)

9

Gorley
Bushes

P

Amberwood Inclosure

Gate
post

Whiteshoot
Bottom

*The water here runs along an artificially straightened channel created in the
19th century to take water from the adjacent reservoir – now Eyeworth Pond –
to the Schultze Gunpowder Factory.*

Miss a turn on the left leading to the pond, and continue straight ahead,
uphill along a tarmac road through more multiple-stemmed, once-coppiced
hollies on the edge of Howen Bushes.

6. At the top of the hill, the Royal Oak pub, a thatched building with smuggling
    traditions, lies a short distance ahead. Otherwise, turn right into the Forestry
    Commission car park.

    *Notice here on the right an old, blackened post box, a relic of gunpowder
    factory days.*

    Immediately take a right fork past another low, Forestry Commission vehicle
    barrier, and continue downhill along the gravelled cycle track beside Gorley
    Bushes.

    *Surface gravel is visible for much of the way along here, and, perhaps not
    surprisingly, there is considerable evidence of relatively small-scale
    extraction.*

7. Follow the cycle track as it eventually bears right where, in the field on the
    right, is the old, gunpowder magazine.

    Ignore a quite wide woodland ride on the right, and continue along the cycle
    track as it enters Islands Thorns Inclosure which, in this section, is an
    attractive mid-19th century oak wood interspersed with occasional conifers.
    Eventually, as the cycle track bears sharply right, pass a track on the left, and
    immediately after, cross the Latchmore Brook at Fritham Bridge.

8. Just beyond the bridge, ignore a turn on the right, and follow the cycle track
    as it bears left, passes through a gap in the wood-bank separating Islands
    Thorns Inclosure from Amberwood Inclosure – marked here by a single, solid
    old gatepost – and then goes right.

9. Leave behind Islands Thorns Inclosure and continue uphill, now with
    Amberwood Inclosure to the left, and to the right, a somewhat more open
    landscape of bracken, hollies, occasional oaks and Scots pines. Ignore a gated
    gravel track on the left.

    *When almost at the top of this quite steep hill, notice on the left a gate and
    path leading into the wood, close to the site of Amberwood Cottage, a property
    abandoned and eventually demolished following the creation of the Second
    World War, Ashley Walk Bombing Range.*

10. Turn right opposite this gate, leave the cycle track and follow another, initially gravelled, track leading across the open heath. *The route from here to the start of Section 13 follows, in the opposite direction, the route used during Walk 1, so details of items seen along the way are not repeated here.*

   Pass on the left an observation shelter and Bronze Age barrow, and miss a number of tracks to right and left as the route continues along the quite broad plateau above Ashley Hole and Islands Thorns Inclosure.

11. Pass a quite wide track on the right, and just beyond on the left, a short distance from the main track, pass a pale, circular area of bare ground with scattered flints and gravel. Follow the track through a gap in the heather, gorse and bracken-topped earthen bank that once surrounded this part of the fragmentation bomb test area, and continue straight ahead.

12. Go through the edge of a group of hollies, gorse and oaks; pass a pronounced track on the right; and ahead, alongside the main track, are the Bronze Age barrows known as The Butts.

13. At a crossroads adjacent to an area of hollies interspersed with gorse and birch, turn right, downhill, eventually alongside a small, barely visible, overgrown old gravel pit. Almost immediately go right then left at a staggered crossroads, and on through Breamore Hat, a small but attractive oak and holly copse.

   Re-enter Islands Thorns Inclosure through a gap in the wood-bank, and pass through a narrow border of Scots pines planted to shelter oak and beech trees within the wood. Follow the now wide track as it bears right, go over a narrow drainage channel, pass a grassy track on the right, and then, as the main track bears left, pass another wider, grassy track on the right.

14. Cross the Latchmore Brook – it is not much wider here than the earlier drainage channel – and immediately after, turn left uphill at a Y-junction. Turn left again, off the main track, to follow a grassy ride that eventually bears round to the right.

   As the track bears to the right, consider a short detour uphill to the right – turn off the track at the far end of a block of beech trees with bare ground below – where can be found the typically hilltop site of Studley Castle.

15. Return to the main track, continue uphill and when close to the inclosure edge, ignore a track on the right at a Y-junction. Pass two aged gateposts beside a gap in the wood-bank, almost immediately take the right fork at the next Y-junction, and follow this track back to the car park.

For the adventurous, for those with a good sense of direction, strong map reading skills and access to an Ordnance Survey map!

Create your own walk by combining parts of this route with elements of your choice from the following selection of connecting or conveniently located nearby routes.

From *New Forest Walks - a time traveller's guide:*

Walk 1   Ashley Walk Bombing Range

Walk 16   Frogham

From *New Forest Walks - a seasonal wildlife guide:*

Walk 1   Godshill Cricket

Walk 3   Fritham

Walk 3
Bramshaw Wood, Black Bush Plain, Shepherds Gutter and Ravens Nest Inclosure

Bramshaw Wood reflects much of the character of England's ancient wildwoods

Setting the scene

This walk starts on the edge of Black Bush Plain, close to the highest point in the New Forest: around 128 metres (420 feet). As the path plunges downhill into Bramshaw Wood, the open heathland of the plain quickly gives way to shaded glades that surely reflect much of the character of England's ancient wildwoods.

Shepherds Gutter, a narrow, picturesque stream, reminds of the days when

Start	Bramble Hill Walk, Forestry Commission car park, across the B3078 Fordingbridge road from Longcross Pond, 3 kilometres (1¾ miles) north-west of Brook - Ordnance Survey map reference SU249153
Distance	6.25 kilometres (4 miles)
Time to allow	1½ - 4 hours
Refreshments	The Lamb Inn, Nomansland, is close to the walk route
Route	'Off the beaten track'
Terrain	Includes a number of quite steep, hilly sections
Rating	3 - in places, quite strenuous walking
Buggies	Not suitable
Railway station	Ashurst (New Forest), 12 kilometres (7½ miles)
Bus service	None
New Forest Tour Bus	Yes
Alternative starts	1) Longcross, Forestry Commission car park, off the minor road to Fritham at Ordnance Survey map reference SU251150 2) Shepards Gutter, Forestry Commission car park - yes, it is spelt like this on the sign! On the walk route beside the minor road between Long Cross and Stock's Cross, south of the Bramble Hill Hotel - Ordnance Survey map reference SU261153 3) Bramshaw Wood, Forestry Commission car park, close to Nomansland - Ordnance Survey map reference SU258173
Forest Holidays Caravan sites and campsites	1) Longbeech, 4 kilometres (2½ miles) 2) Ocknell, 5 kilometres (3 miles)

sheep were regularly put out to graze on the open lands of the New Forest; whilst Ravens Nest Inclosure recalls the 18th century presence of these huge, black birds and their bulky, tree-top nests.

Along the way

Common of Pasture - ponies, cattle, donkeys and mules

Black Bush Plain and nearby Longcross Pond are favourite haunts of local New Forest ponies. Indeed, when thinking of the New Forest, it's probably the free-ranging ponies, cattle, donkeys and occasional mules that first come to mind. These, though, are not wild animals, for they are owned by local people, by New Forest commoners who, through occupation of land with associated common rights, are entitled to put out their stock on the open Forest.

Donkeys sheltering from winter weather

Tradition has it that these rights were first granted by William the Conqueror in the late 11th century when, fresh from victory at the Battle of Hastings, he set aside as a Royal hunting ground the land he called *Nova Foresta*, the place now known as the New Forest. William, it is often said, prevented the local inhabitants from enclosing their properties for fear that fencing would hinder the run of the deer, and in return, granted permission for domestic animals to wander outside the holdings.

But common rights do, in fact, pre-date creation of the hunting ground. for these entitlements were then already in use by many hard-working men with few assets to call their own, men who depended on shared access to common land that often was of too poor a quality to be of interest to the powerful landowners of the time.

Today, common of pasture, the entitlement to put out stock, is the most widely exercised of these rights. Numbers of animals vary annually – in recent years, there have been around 4,700 ponies, 2,400 cattle, 125 donkeys, and mules too few to count.

The other main, currently exercised rights are common of mast, which is the right to put out pigs; and common of fuelwood, which entitles holders to wood for the fire.

Common of Pasture for Sheep, Common of Marl and Common of Turbary - rights of old

Sheep nowadays are rarely seen on the open lands of the New Forest, but Shepherds Gutter, a tiny stream that rises near Black Bush Plain and flows south-east towards Brook, reminds of the related common right. Late 19th century maps also have Shepherds Copse and Sheepwash Green in the vicinity, and there's also the Lamb Inn at nearby Nomansland to cement the local connection.

The right, common of pasture for sheep, is attached to former monastic property in the south-east of the area, and to a number of fields in the extreme north-west. In recent years, up to 150 animals have been depastured.

Two other, once popular common rights are now no longer used at all. Common of marl allowed for the extraction of lime-rich

The Turfcutters Arms: a reminder of common of turbary

clay for use as a fertiliser, whilst common of turbary provided for peaty turf to be cut for fuel. Marl was eventually superseded by modern alternatives, and common of turbary entered the history books following the increased availability of coal early in the 20th century. Disused marl pits are reasonably widespread, particularly in the south of the Forest, although little evidence of turf cutting remains. The Turfcutters Arms at East Boldre is, however, a reminder of this ancient right.

The Pits - gravel, clay, sand, marl and more

The surface of the Bramble Hill Walk car park is considerably below the level of the surrounding land, and that is not surprising for it is located in an old gravel pit, just one of many that will be encountered during this and other New Forest walks.

Indeed, small-scale gravel pits, many dating back to at least the 18th and 19th centuries, can be found sprinkled about the New Forest wherever suitable deposits occur reasonably close to the surface. The gravel was, no doubt, used in the construction of local turnpike and other roads, and latterly, to improve woodland tracks needed to take out felled timber. Similarly, evidence of small-scale clay, sand and marl pits – the latter often floristically rich – is also frequently encountered, whilst signs of ironstone and sandstone extraction occur much more locally.

(Notice during Section 3 of this walk, the bumps and hollows of an old, disused pit cut into the hillside on the edge of Bramshaw Wood. Despite close proximity to a number of old gravel workings, there is no obvious evidence here of gravel below the accumulated deposits of leaf mould and other detritus. The presence of mature trees, including a large pollard beech, does, though, suggest that the pit was in use well over 300 years ago.)

The site of 17th century clay extraction close to Clayhill Heath, near Lyndhurst

Ravens Nest Inclosure - a story of persecution with a happy ending

One of the earliest New Forest inclosures, Ravens Nest Inclosure dates back to 1775 and is now an attractive mixture of conifers and broadleaved trees. Ravens, the largest members of the crow family, presumably bred here in those far-off days, but by the mid-19th century, after prolonged persecution by gamekeepers, farmers and egg collectors, and a fashion for keeping the young as pets, they had disappeared as breeders from much of lowland Britain – until recently, the last New Forest breeding record was in 1858.

Now, though, the raven is back and doing fairly well, largely as a result of reduced persecution throughout its range. Re-colonisation is underway and the birds' spectacular late winter and spring-time display flights can once more be seen above the woods, and their gruff, far-carrying croaks heard amidst the clamour of smaller birds.

A quiet corner of Ravens Nest Inclosure

The Route

1. Follow in a clockwise direction a quite wide, grassy track running between the car park and road, before going diagonally across Black Bush Plain, heading towards the left-hand end of a small copse mid-way across the heath.

   When close to the copse, notice to the left of the path a number of eroded Bronze Age barrows, part of a well-spread, thirteen-strong group. Many have been badly mutilated by past excavation, a sacrilegious act perpetrated on what, after all, are ancient burial sites.

2. Pass through the edge of the copse, and at an indistinct crossroads, ignore a minor fork in the track going away to the right. Immediately upon reaching Black Bush Hat, an area of ancient, unenclosed woodland, ignore another indistinct minor track going straight ahead.

   Continue round to the right, alongside the wood, for around 75 metres, and take the next left fork at a Y-junction.

3. Go straight ahead at two consecutive crossroads of tracks and continue on until the track goes downhill into Bramshaw Wood, close here to Two Beeches Bottom. Pass an old, disused woodland pit on the right, and again continue straight ahead, downhill for around 500 metres, passing by minor tracks to left and right.

4. Take the left-hand fork at a branch in the main track - this is not particularly noticeable in summer when vegetation partly obscures the way, but should it be missed, the right-hand fork leads down to the same valley-bottom stream.

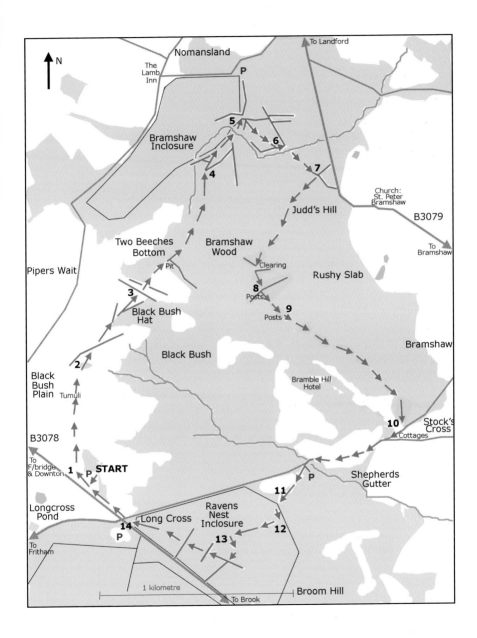

Pass a minor track on the left and shortly after, turn right at a T-junction alongside the prominent, moss-clad wood-bank that, with fencing atop, prevented access by browsing animals to the saplings of Bramshaw Inclosure following the 1829 creation of this plantation.

Pass a prominent track coming in from the right, and cross a small stream in the valley bottom. Beware, there is no bridge here, and after rain, the water can get quite swollen. In summer, however, the stream is often dry.

5. Continue uphill and after around 75 metres, turn right at a staggered crossroads, just before a quite wide track joins from the left, from within Bramshaw Inclosure.

    The Lamb Inn at Nomansland is around 0.75 kilometres (½ mile) from here. To reach it, do not take the right turn just mentioned, but instead continue further uphill, keeping parallel to the inclosure wood-bank on the left. Go straight through Bramshaw Wood car park, turn left along a tarmac road, and the pub is ahead, close to a T-junction.

    Otherwise, after walking a few paces across the short-cropped turf of what is a woodland clearing, turn half-right, ignore a prominent track on the right, and continue straight ahead, at first up a gentle gradient with, eventually, tree roots sprawling across the quite narrow path as it clings to the hillside.

6. Pass a track joining from back to the right, and after 50 metres, turn right at a crossroads to go over a narrow, open valley. Re-cross the stream, this time at a bridge, and continue straight ahead up a gentle incline.

7. Turn right at a crossroads, just before the top of the hill is reached.

    The track straight ahead at this crossroads leads to a minor road, the B3079, near to the church of St. Peter, Bramshaw. Turn right along this road to reach the church, which is around 500 metres away, set on a hillock overlooking the road. It dates back in part to the early 13th century, although much was re-built in brick in 1829.

    Otherwise, after turning right, continue up an incline, following the quite wide main track. Eventually go downhill for a short distance, and straight across a small, grassy clearing – ignore here minor tracks to right and left, before starting up another gentle incline.

8. Shortly after the clearing, turn right at a T-junction. Almost immediately go left at another T-junction, this beside two old, disused wooden posts that indicate the site of fencing erected in the 1960s – as described for Eyeworth Wood in Walk 2. Continue uphill for a short distance.

9. Pass between two further disused trackside posts, and follow the track as it bears left and goes slightly downhill for a while before again resuming a steady uphill climb.

    Eventually continue down a predominantly gentle incline before emerging after around 800 metres onto a minor road opposite two cottages.

10. Turn right along this road and pass on the right, a drive leading to the Bramble Hill Hotel, built on the site of an old lodge. Eventually cross Shepherds Gutter, a narrow, gravel-bottomed New Forest stream.

    After a very short distance, turn left into the Forestry Commission car park and immediately go half-right, diagonally uphill across an area of grass – keep alongside the woodland edge on the left.

11. Continue straight ahead into the wood, following what initially is a shallow, sunken track. Almost immediately pass through a quite wide gap in the Ravens Nest Inclosure wood-bank, and turn left to follow alongside this low bank which here is topped by a number of enormous beech pollards and maiden trees.

12. Turn right almost immediately, just before a tiny stream is reached, and go uphill, parallel to the water course – note, though, that dense bracken in summer can almost obscure sight of the stream. Continue half-right alongside a fence surrounding on the left an area recently cleared of trees.

13. Follow the fence-line as it goes 90 degrees to the left, and, where the fence goes left again, turn right opposite a gate to follow along a quite wide track. After a short distance, turn right at a crossroad of tracks to continue through the wood on a course running broadly parallel to the B3078 Brook – Fordingbridge road.

    Go straight ahead at two indistinct crossroads, and emerge from the trees close to a road junction.

14. Turn right along the road, go over the minor road leading back towards the Bramble Hill Hotel, and the car park is straight ahead on the right.

Start	Millyford Bridge, Forestry Commission car park on the minor road from Emery Down to Bolderwood and Linwood - Ordnance Survey map reference SU268078
Distance	4.5 kilometres (2¾ miles) Shorter walk: 3.5 kilometres (2 miles)
Time to allow	1 - 2¾ hours
Refreshments	The New Forest Inn, Emery Down, is close to the start of the walk
Route	Along readily visible tracks
Terrain	Mainly on level ground, but with a small number of gentle gradients
Rating	1 - easy walking
Buggies	Except after rain, the route in late spring and summer is usually suitable for sturdy buggies, although the ground can still be a little wet and rutted in places, particularly in Section 5 of the route
Railway station	1) Ashurst (New Forest), 7.25 kilometres (4½ miles) 2) Beaulieu Road, 8.75 kilometres (5½ miles) 3) Brockenhurst, 9.75 kilometres (6 miles)
Bus service	Bluestar and National Express serve nearby Lyndhurst
New Forest Tour Bus	Serves nearby Lyndhurst
Alternative starts	None
Forest Holidays Caravan sites and campsites	1) Matley Wood, 6.75 kilometres (4¼ miles) 2) Denny Wood, 7.25 kilometres (4½ miles) 3) Ashurst, 7.25 kilometres (4½ miles) 4) Hollands Wood, 8.5 kilometres (5¼ miles)

Walk 4
Millyford Bridge; Highland Water; Holmhill, Wooson's Hill and Holidays Hill Inclosures

Highland Water in autumn

Setting the scene

Situated 3.25 kilometres (2 miles) west of Lyndhurst, Millyford Bridge at the start of this walk carries a minor road over Highland Water, a delightfully steep-banked, gravel-bottomed New Forest stream.

Ancient, unenclosed woodland quickly gives way to Holmhill Inclosure, created in the early 19th century on the site of a much earlier planting – the inclosure now features many fine, mature oak, beech and sweet chestnut trees. Wooson's Hill Inclosure, visited later in the walk, dates to around 1829, and Holidays Hill Inclosure to 1811.

The Portuguese Fireplace is passed along the way, and so, half-hidden by vegetation, is a cutting through which ran a First World War narrow gauge railway used to transport timber to a nearby sawmill. An abandoned charcoal burners' pit provides a further reminder of how these woodlands have for centuries been exploited by man.

Along the way

Holmhill Inclosure - a tale of two plantings

Out for a ride in Holmhill Inclosure

Holmhill Inclosure, created in 1815 on the site of ancient woodland interspersed with open areas, probably of heath, lawn and wetter ground, also took in much of a considerably older enclosure laid out in 1670.

One of three unsuccessful attempts to combat anticipated shortages of timber needed for Navy shipbuilding – the other two were at Holidays Hill and Aldridge Hill – part of the old enclosure's hexagonal outline is shown on the walk sketch map. Today, few of the original trees remain, but the substantial surrounding earthen woodbank can still be seen.

Highland Water - 'improvement' and restoration

Highland Water is one of the most attractive New Forest streams. Clear, clean, high-banked and gravel-bottomed, it is free of man's pollutants, but not man's influence. Look out during this walk for meanders cut off from the main flow, meanders that often still fill with water after heavy rains. And notice, also,

Highland Water, with apparatus to monitor the flow

sections of the stream that are just too straight to be natural. Both are indicators of 19th and 20th century 'improvements', of stream straightening, widening and deepen-ing in attempts to hurry the water through, so as to reduce flooding and improve the timber growing and grazing potential of the adjacent land.

But in the process of 'improvement', important damp woodland habitats have been badly affected, habitats that now are relatively rare in Britain and the rest of Europe; whilst gravel beds, important for spawning trout, have been reduced in size and quality.

Recently, however, some of the isolated meanders have been linked back to the parent stream, and other restoration works completed, offering hope of a return to the characteristics of old.

Stag Parks - vague outlines on the ground, and still something of a mystery

A little to the north of the walk route, within Highland Water Inclosure, is the site of an old Stag Park, a rectangular-shaped enclosure with external ditch.

One of three such parks shown in the late 18th century on Richardson, King and Driver's map of the New Forest – the others were in Denny Wood and close to Rhinefield House – its exact purpose remains unclear, although it has been suggested that all were created in the late 17th century to hold red deer recently

Red deer: the Stag Park inhabitants?

imported from France, an introduction that also necessitated the extension of New Park, near Brockenhurst.

Earthwork remains can still be seen in all three locations, although the site in Highland Water Inclosure has relatively recently been close-planted with conifers, obscuring much below the rapidly growing branches.

Portuguese Fireplace - wartime help in the woods

This substantial, isolated flint-faced chimney breast and fireplace seems somewhat out of place in the New Forest, but its history is very much in keeping with that of the surrounding woodlands for it recalls the First World War presence of Canadian and Portuguese workers who helped to harvest substantial amounts of local timber for war-time use in French camps and war-torn trenches.

Retained from a Portuguese cookhouse, the fireplace serves as a memorial to the men who lived and worked here; whilst adjacent bumps

The Portuguese Fireplace

and hollows mark the site of a Canadian Forestry Corps camp. Heywood Sumner, though, writing not long after hostilities ceased, recalled somewhat ungraciously, beautiful thickets of old holly trees on nearby Mogshade Hill, damaged by fire in 1918 in an incident 'remembered as a war-time, careless mishap, to the discredit of over-seas woodmen.'

Two squirrels - the introduction of the grey and the eventual loss of the red

It can be difficult to walk for any length of time in New Forest woodlands without seeing or hearing a grey squirrel. They are almost everywhere, sometimes in relatively large numbers. But it was not always so, for the infinitely more attractive red squirrel is the native species, whilst the grey squirrel is present only following progressive introduction to Britain from the eastern United States, starting in around 1876.

Indeed, so formerly widespread were red squirrels that they were viewed as enemies of the forester, animals whose numbers had to be controlled; or they were killed for the pot; or taken for sport using stout sticks with a piece of lead attached to the end. John Wise, writing in the 19th century, noted bags of 100 or more brought home and baked in pies; whilst Gerald Lascelles, New Forest Deputy Surveyor from 1880 until 1914, commented that 'great congregations of squirrel hunters about Christmas time all met together in the evening, at one or other of the local public houses, and enjoyed great suppers of "squirrel pie", the product of the day's amusement.' And in 1889 alone, over 2,000 were reported shot.

Grey squirrels had, however, reached the New Forest by the 1930s, and within a few years the red squirrels were gone, unable to live side-by-side with their larger cousins. Today the nearest red squirrel populations survive in splendid isolation on the Isle of Wight and Brownsea Island.

Red squirrels disappeared shortly after the arrival of grey squirrels

The Route

1. Leave the car park along a gravel track leading directly away from the road. Cross a small, inconspicuous bridge – it has a single low, moss-covered parapet – over a narrow side-stream that is often dry in summer, then cross a wooden, railed bridge over the main river. *On both sides of the path here is a broad, often water-filled meander cut off from the main flow.*

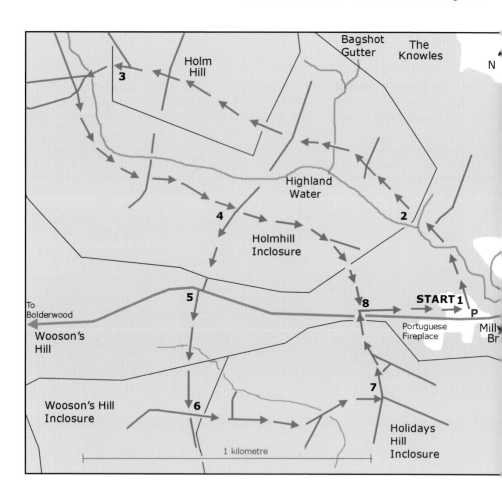

Pass on the left a number of aged beech trees and probably older hollies, cross a small clearing and go through a gate into Holmhill Inclosure.

2. Continue along the gravel track, pass over a crossroads where a grassy ride intersects the main track, and cross a small bridge over Bagshot Gutter.
    Continue straight ahead at the next crossroads – where another grassy ride intersects the track – with immediately on the left, an area of regenerating woodland fenced to exclude deer and commoners' stock.
    Midway along this fence-line, immediately before the start of similar fencing on the right-hand side of the track, the route passes through the substantial earthen wood-bank constructed around the original 1670 enclosure.

Go straight ahead again where the next grassy ride intersects the track, and after about 100 metres, take the left fork at a Y-junction.

3. Follow the track downhill and almost immediately pass again through the 1670 wood-bank. Re-cross Highland Water at a bridge, and continue along the track as it bears round to the left, ignoring here a grassy ride going straight ahead, uphill.

    Almost immediately, where the main gravel track swings round to the right, turn left down a lesser used gravel track running parallel to the river. After a further 450 metres, continue straight ahead where a grassy ride intersects the track.

4. After another 400 metres, turn right at a crossroads and continue along an overgrown gravel track – there is little gravel along the tracks to the left and straight ahead here.

    To take the shorter walk, continue straight ahead at the crossroads; ignore a grassy ride on the left; and shortly after, leave the inclosure through a pedestrian gate.

    Notice on the left, 8 metres, or so, beyond the gate and on a course almost parallel to the path, a bracken-filled cutting bordered by moss-encrusted banks - in places, it is almost 2 metres deep and 2 metres wide. This was part of the route of a First World War narrow gauge railway associated with a sawmill near Millyford Bridge. It's difficult now, of course, to imagine steam trains running through this peaceful part of the New Forest.

    Continue uphill across a small, grassy clearing, and then go straight ahead to reach the minor road close to the Portuguese Fireplace at the start of Section 8.

    Otherwise, when 250 metres along the overgrown gravel track, go through a gate out of the inclosure. Continue along what is now a grassy ride, and just ahead, beyond a vehicle barrier, is the minor road.

5. Cross over the road, turn right and immediately left down a narrow grassy path – this, in effect, is a staggered junction. Continue virtually straight ahead along the path, down a gentle gradient into a wooded valley.

    Cross an un-railed stone bridge over a narrow stream; after a short distance, go through a gate set in a gap in a prominent, moss-clad wood-bank; and enter Wooson's Hill Inclosure. After 200 metres, reach a crossroads and turn left along a little-used gravel track.

6. Follow this track into Holidays Hill Inclosure. Ignore a narrow path on the left, then another on the right, and continue downhill for a short distance to again cross the stream.

7. Reach another crossroads and turn left along a substantial gravel track. After around 150 metres, take the left-hand fork at a Y-junction, continue straight ahead and go through a gate to reach the road.

8. Turn right and walk beside the road.

After a short distance, consider taking a detour to the right, alongside the inclosure wood-bank, where after around 25 metres, on the left can be seen the eroded, circular earthen rim and leaf-filled interior of a 6 metre diameter charcoal burners' pit. The presence on the rim of an old pollard beech suggests a 17th century, or earlier, origin, as in 1698 pollarding of timber trees in the New Forest was forbidden by Act of Parliament.

Pass the Portuguese Fireplace, and continue along the road for a short distance to reach the Millyford Bridge car park.

On the left-hand side of the road, immediately before the turn for the car park, can be found a quite large, rectangular concrete block mostly concealed amongst a group of small trees. On the right-hand side of the road, immediately after the turn, are concrete bases and other hardstandings. First and Second World War sawmills were located here.

For the adventurous, for those with a good sense of direction, strong map reading skills and access to an Ordnance Survey map!
Create your own walk by combining parts of this route with elements of your choice from the following selection of connecting or conveniently located nearby routes.

From *New Forest Walks – a seasonal wildlife guide:*
Walk 11   Bolderwood Deer Sanctuary

Walk 5
Lyndhurst Golf Course and
the old Race Ground

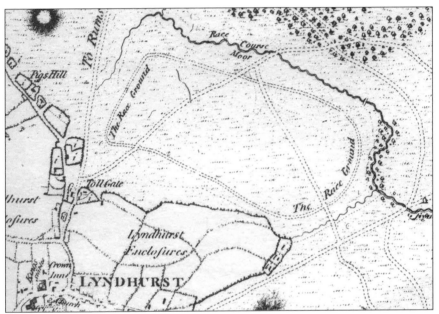

Lyndhurst Race Ground, as shown on the 1814 Richardson, King, Driver and Driver map

Setting the scene

Not far from Lyndhurst village centre, this quite short walk route passes around the edge of the local golf course, an extensive area of grassland ever-popular with commoners' ponies and cattle, and a flourishing population of seemingly quite tame, wild rabbits.

Bordered for much of the way by alder carr and ancient, unenclosed woodland, the golf course is particularly well-used during summer weekends, so walkers might prefer to visit at other times.

Start	The New Forest Centre, situated in Lyndhurst's main, village centre car park - Ordnance Survey map reference SU300081
Distance	4 kilometres (2½ miles)
Time to allow	1 - 2½ hours
Refreshments	There are a number of pubs in Lyndhurst
Route	Along readily visible tracks
Terrain	On level ground throughout
Rating	1 - easy walking
Buggies	Not suitable
Railway station	1) Ashurst (New Forest), 4 kilometres (2½ miles) 2) Beaulieu Road, 5.5 kilometres (3½ miles) 3) Brockenhurst, 6.25 kilometres (4 miles)
Bus service	Bluestar and National Express
New Forest Tour Bus	Yes
Alternative start	A lay-by on the A337 Lyndhurst - Cadnam road, opposite the Police Station at Ordnance Survey map reference SU299088, offers an alternative start for those entering Lyndhurst on this road. Access is through/over an adjacent narrow stile
Forest Holidays Caravan sites and campsites	1) Matley Wood, 3.5 kilometres (2 miles) 2) Denny Wood, 4 kilometres (2½ miles) 3) Ashurst, 4 kilometres (2½ miles) 4) Hollands Wood, 5 kilometres (3 miles)

Along the way

Turnpike roads - from primitive tracks to the start of a modern road system

Although many early roads were not much more than dusty or muddy tracks, depending on the season, from the first years of the 18th century, main through routes were increasingly improved by newly formed turnpike trusts. The trusts charged for the privilege of usage, and in return maintained the roads, replacing the previously haphazard system of parish maintenance. Roadside milestones were provided, and strategically placed toll gates acted as payment collection points.

Lyndhurst enjoyed the services of three such trusts:
- The Lymington, Lyndhurst and Rumbridge Turnpike Trust, 1765
- From 1753 to 1870, the Salisbury, Landford, Ower and Eling Turnpike Trust, whose route from 1771 included a branch road into Lyndhurst along what is now the A337 from Cadnam – the road taken during this walk
- The Christchurch and Lyndhurst Turnpike Trust, 1841.

Milestones can still be seen beside each of the routes, whilst two of the cottages used for toll collection on the 1771 branch road are passed during the early stages of this walk – they are the thatched cottage close to the turn for Forest Gardens; and black and white Turnpike Cottage, opposite Racecourse View.

The tolls were, though, originally collected 2 kilometres (1¼ miles) outside the village, not far from the turn for Minstead, but by 1789 the gate had moved to the site of Turnpike Cottage, and by 1834 to the thatched cottage, which ensured that travellers from nearby Pikeshill had to pay. Understandably unhappy, residents successfully petitioned the Trust and the gate was moved back to Turnpike Cottage.

Turnpike Cottage is opposite Racecourse View

These and other turnpike roads were eventually put out of business by the 19th century coming of the railways.

Lyndhurst Race Ground - fun and frolics at the races

Perhaps surprisingly, Lyndhurst was once the home of a substantial racecourse, located to the north-east of the village, largely on the site of the present golf course. The date of the first race is uncertain, but by the late 18th century the course had already given its name to what then was known as Race Course Moor.

Golfers enjoy a round on the site of the old race ground

An almost rectangular circuit, the course measured around 1 kilometre (just over ½ mile) by 0.5 kilometre (¹/₃ mile) and served as an important meeting place for those who came to enjoy a day's flat racing, to pit their wits against the local bookmakers and to participate in the accompanying fair-day attractions. Not only horses raced here, though, for George Rose of the nearby Cuffnells estate was the owner of a racing ox that apparently performed admirably.

Racing ceased in around 1880, in 1890 part of the old course was taken over by the New Forest Golf Club, and from 1922 until after the Second World War, the New Forest pony sales and accompanying fair took place on the remainder of the site.

Memorable oaks - just two of many

Tucked away within the woods a little beyond the north-west corner of the old Race Ground, one of the

The Knightwood Oak, a well-known New Forest pollard

New Forest's grandest oak trees looks down on passers-by, just as it has done for centuries past. Measured by Chris Read during a mid-1990s survey, the trunk's girth was a mighty 6.7 metres (22 feet), sufficient to rank it as the fifth largest New Forest oak found at that time. Probably in excess of 400 years old, the tree had stretched the tape in the late 1970s to a slightly more modest 6.6 metres (21½ feet), a mere 0.6 metres (2 feet) behind the biggest of them all: the Knightwood Oak.

Referred to by John Wise in the early 1860s as 'the famous Knyghtwood Oak' and shown on the 1870 Ordnance Survey map as the 'Queen of the Forest', this old tree continues to attract visitors to its humble woodland site 4 kilometres (2½ miles) south-west of Lyndhurst. It is said to be around 600 years old and now boasts a girth of about 7.5 metres (24½ feet). The presence of multiple trunks at a little above head-height shows that it has on at least one occasion been pollarded, cut back at that level to encourage new shoots to grow safely out of reach of hungry deer and commoners' stock, shoots that would have been used, for example, as domestic firewood and charcoal burners' fuel.

But whilst pollarding might seem brutal, trees treated in this way did not usually produce timber of suitable size and shape for ship building, and so were spared the far more final axe taken to so many maiden – un-pollarded – oaks when, from the early 17th century to the early 19th century, the New Forest's unenclosed woodlands provided substantial amounts of material for use in the construction of the naval vessels that laid much of the foundations for Britain's contemporary power and wealth.

Drainage channels - man-made attempts to create conditions conducive to grazing

Many parts of the New Forest, including areas around the edge of the golf course, can be very wet

Yellow iris plants thrive in one of the drainage channels passed during this walk

underfoot. Indeed, where bogs have formed, commoners' stock occas-ionally get stuck and require rescue; although gone are the days when 'men, horses and carts were swallowed up', as one late 19th century writer reported, for drainage schemes have had a significant impact on the height of the water table.

Use of drainage channels, for example, initially on a relatively small scale, increased in the second half of the 19th century and more significantly so following the New Forest Act 1949, which contained provisions specifically designed to increase and maintain grazing for the stock.

Yet despite having often replaced small, meandering, entirely natural streams; many of these straight, originally quite deep canals have assumed a pleasing appearance and provide a significant resource for wildlife. In recent years, however, in attempts to turn back the clock and produce landscape and wildlife conditions of old, a number of drainage channels have been filled with earth, and new, shallow stream beds created. The success, or otherwise, of these initiatives remains to be seen!

The Route

1. Leave the New Forest Centre via the adjacent car park exit leading to the High Street. Cross the road at the pedestrian crossing, turn left, and then right at the traffic lights, into Romsey Road.

   Keep to the right-hand side of Romsey Road. Pass Wellands Road on the right, King's Close on the left, Empress Road and Queen's Parade on the right, and Forest Gardens on the left.

   Continue past Gales Green and Turnpike Cottage, both on the left. Just beyond the last buildings on the right are the extensive grasslands now largely occupied by the golf course. Turn right here into Racecourse View and access to the grasslands is through a gate on the left, a short distance along the road.

2. From the gate, go half-left to meet at the end of a drainage channel, the fence bordering the main road. A path running alongside the fence goes past the lay-by alternative start point stile.

   From the lay-by stile, walk half-right for a short distance over the grassland, pass through a narrow gap in the trees ahead – the gap is almost mid-way between the main road and a birch-clad hillock with bench at its base – and turn left to skirt the golf course.

3. Keep to the edge of the golf course by walking close to the trees on your left, remembering to take extra care if golf is in progress. Reach a strip of

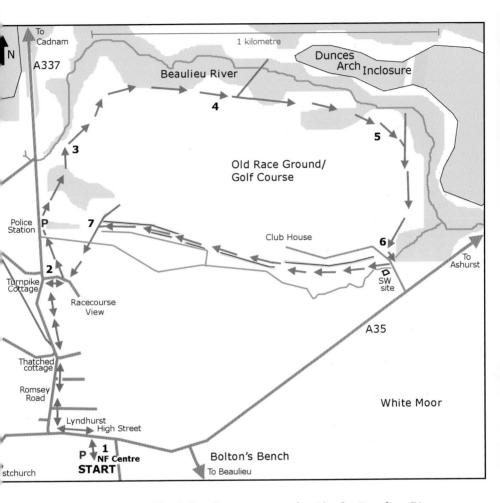

primarily alder woodland that has grown up beside the Beaulieu River –
which has its source just across the main road, not far from the police
station.

Go right to follow the woodland edge over ground that in the 18th
century was known as Race Course Moor.

4. Keep to the edge of the woodland; pass a gravel track on the left leading
   into the trees; and shortly after, pass to the left of a golf course green
   skirting a clump of ancient, coppiced hollies with, just beyond, an area of
   heath and rough grassland.

5. Continue along the edge of the golf course; and pass another turning on the left just as you begin to go round to the right, following the line of a low bank or the nearby woodland edge.

6. Keep to the left of another golf course green, and upon reaching a tarmac road, turn left and then immediately right (just before a small, fenced Southern Water site) to initially follow beside a narrow stream through a straggle of woodland.

   After a short distance, follow the path along the ridge of an earthen bank, one of two that intermittently run parallel to each other 15 metres, or so, apart, almost from the A35 to the A337.

   It is tempting to imagine that these once bordered the old race course, but they are simply spoil-heaps thrown up in the late 1930s when construction of a Lyndhurst bypass started. The project was, however, soon halted following strong local objections to the proposed route.

   When trees block the way ahead, continue along a path running along the right-hand bank before emerging onto an area of grass and gorse. Keep going straight ahead, now between the two banks, until a T-junction of tracks is reached.

7. To return to Racecourse View, turn left, cross an almost adjacent small bridge, and the gate alongside the road will be seen across the grassland.

   To reach the roadside lay-by, turn right at the T-junction, and then immediately left to follow woodland edge for a short distance before crossing the grassland close to the road.

Walk 6

Ashurst: Busketts, Lodgehill, Ironshill and Busketts Lawn Inclosures

Setting the scene

Explore attractive woodlands fanning out from the edge of Ashurst, providing mile-upon-mile of enjoyable walking along gravel cycle tracks. Located conveniently close to Ashurst (New Forest) railway station, the start of the walk is also well-served by Bluestar buses, whilst those arriving by car should use a small, public car park located near the Happy Cheese pub, beside the A35 – if parking space is not available there, alternatives can usually be found nearby.

Access to the woods is over a stile, also adjacent to the A35. Please note, though, that for much of the year, the ground between stile and cycle track – a distance of around 800 metres (½ mile) – can be wet and muddy.

A quiet track in Lodgehill Inclosure

Start	A stile beside the A35, Ashurst to Lyndhurst road, at the bottom of the hill leading over the railway bridge - Ordnance Survey map reference SU333102. (The stile is set quite well-back from the road, opposite the garden of The New Forest pub. It is adjacent both to the end of the railings running uphill alongside the roadside footpath, and to a road sign for Woodlands)
Distance	5.5 kilometres (3½ miles) Shorter walk: 3.5 kilometres (2 miles)
Time to allow	1½ - 3½ hours
Refreshments	The New Forest and the Happy Cheese are both close to the start of the walk
Route	Along readily visible tracks
Terrain	Mainly on level ground, but with a small number of gentle gradients
Rating	1 - easy walking
Buggies	Suitable for sturdy buggies when the route is accessed from Woodlands Road
Railway station	Ashurst (New Forest), adjacent to the start of the walk
Bus service	Bluestar
New Forest Tour Bus	Yes
Alternative start	Details are contained in the 'Setting the scene' section
Forest Holidays Caravan sites and campsites	Ashurst, adjacent to the route

Alternative access, with relatively limited parking space, is available along two buggy-friendly cycle tracks leading from nearby Woodlands Road – they are marked in blue on the sketch map. However, as there is no footpath beside Woodlands Road, pedestrians coming from the A35 must walk along the side of the road or on the grass verge. Motorists who park by the cycle track gates should take care not to obstruct access for Forestry Commission and other vehicles, and should follow instructions given on signs placed by the Forestry Commission.

Along the way

A wonderful old map and the second (1808) Act of Parliament to authorise creation of timber plantations

Produced by Thomas Richardson, William King and Abraham and William Driver, the map shown here, part of the 1814 second edition of the first accurate, large scale map of the New Forest, opens a fascinating window on Ironshill Inclosure as it was in the late 18th century.

But for many local people, the map was of doubtful benefit. Originally surveyed in 1787 and published in 1789, production was commissioned to

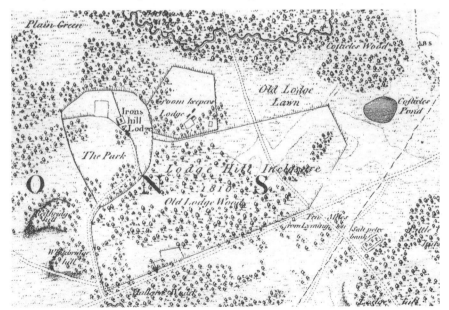

The 1814 Richardson, King, Driver and Driver map shows newly created Lodgehill Inclosure, but not the contemporary Ironshill Inclosure

accompany the New Forest element of a national review set up to investigate ways of improving Crown land management and revenues, particularly relating to the old forests that, with their own officers, courts, laws, and shared interests with holders of common rights, were seen as ripe for change.

Disafforestation – the break up of the forests through land allocations to the Crown, and to private individuals in recognition of their common rights – was in many places the favoured outcome, but in the New Forest, where the threat of disafforestation had subsided following a failed attempt in 1792, an increase in the area set aside for trees was preferred, and authorised in 1808 by a second Act for the Increase and Preservation of Timber – the first had been in 1698 (details are included with Walk 1) and the next would be in 1851 (see Walk 9).

Much to the dismay of local commoners, however, stock, as ever, were to be excluded from the new inclosures until the trees were sufficiently well-grown to withstand damage caused by browsing animals; and even when re-admitted, only limited accessible vegetation would be available on which they could feed.

Ironshill, Lodgehill and Costicles were amongst the inclosures subsequently created. The second edition of the map showed many of the new woodlands, and of course, disafforestation never did happen, although the prospect was to resurface again later in the 19th century.

Common of Fuelwood - wood for the home hearth

When walking through woodland inclosures, look out for timber stacked neatly by the ride-sides, for this will often have been cut and set aside by the Forestry Commission for collection by local people entitled to stipulated amounts of wood for the fire.

Sometimes known as estovers, common of fuelwood is an ancient common right although its operation has changed considerably since the days when commoners

A commoner cutting ride-side fuelwood

were largely at liberty to cut their own wood from wherever they pleased, often with relatively little supervision. The Crown has also steadily bought-out the entitlement, so usage has significantly fallen – in 1883 there were 130 fuelwood rights, whilst by 1983 these had reduced to just below 100.

Ironshill Lodge and Ironshill Inclosure - a royal residence and Napoleonic prison

Ironshill Lodge stands in its own grounds in the midst of the woods. The original underkeeper's lodge constructed here in 1609 was rebuilt in the late 18th century and has since had substantial later additions. The name suggests a link with ironstone or an iron foundry.

Fuelwood stacked by the ride-side in Ironshill Inclosure

But this is not the only lodge to have been situated hereabouts, for in the mid-18th century, using funds provided by the Treasury for repairs to the original building, a master keeper's lodge was surreptitiously built on the hill to the right of the current gravel track through the inclosure. This later became the official residence of Her Royal Highness Princess Sophia of Gloucester, whose father, the Duke of Gloucester, was Lord Warden of the New Forest; and was subsequently used as a prison during the Napoleonic Wars before eventually being demolished.

The relative status of the two lodges was well-illustrated on the 1814 map, which simply marked the original building and grounds as Groom keepers Lodge – underkeepers were also known as groom keepers – whilst the later property, known then as Ironshill Lodge, was set within a far larger estate marked in the fashion of the times as The Park.

In 1810, Ironshill Inclosure was created on the site of the newer lodge, and planted with trees. Although now primarily mature beech and oak woodland, conifers are also present and so are hollies, hawthorns and once-coppiced hazels.

Four other woodland inclosures - a bit of history

In addition to Ironshill Inclosure, this walk passes through Lodgehill Inclosure (which also dates back to 1810), Costicles Inclosure (1829), Busketts Inclosure (1864) and Busketts Lawn Inclosure (also 1864). Although originally planted to satisfy a desire for timber, all are now widely appreciated for their amenity and wildlife value.

Costicles Inclosure follows the boundary of what in the late 18th century was known as Costicles Wood, an area similar in character to the New Forest's other ancient, unenclosed woodlands. Many, if not all, of the old trees would have been felled to make way for the new plantation oaks and beeches, many of which remain today as fine, mature specimens.

Busketts Lawn Inclosure was planted, quite literally, on Busketts Lawn and on Old Lodge Lawn, both of which would most likely have been extensive grasslands or heathlands, interspersed with hawthorns, blackthorns, crab apple trees, hollies and gorse – the very

Early spring in Costicles Inclosure

essence of the old Forest. The inclosure is now an attractive mixture of broadleaved trees and conifers with, in places along Bartley Water and the ride-sides, impressively enormous Douglas firs.

Busketts Inclosure was also planted on open ground, whilst Lodgehill Inclosure was previously occupied, in part, by Old Lodge Wood. Both now contain a mixture of broadleaves and conifers.

Bartley Water - home of kingfishers and grey wagtails

Writing in the early 1860s, John Wise suggested that one of the best ways to see the New Forest in all its glorious variety was 'to follow the course of one of its streams, to make it a friend and companion, and go wherever it goes'.

And that is still often good advice, although since the planting of Busketts Lawn Inclosure, it does not apply to Bartley Water which today flows almost entirely through woodland before leaving the Forest and continuing on its way. Nor in many places is it easy to follow the

Kingfishers sometimes breed along Bartley Water

stream's every twist and turn through sometimes dense undergrowth, even though in recent years much adjacent vegetation has been cleared so as to let in more light, which in turn encourages the growth of brambles and other wild flowers, and consequently provides improved habitat for butterflies.

The Route

1. Cross the stile at the start of the route and enter Busketts Inclosure. Follow the indistinct path that goes directly away from the road, across an adjacent wide, grassy, somewhat overgrown ride running parallel to the road.

   Pass through a very narrow corridor of trees, and immediately after, turn left along another wide, grassy ride overhung with trees – this is around 25 metres from the stile.

   Eventually pass yet another grassy ride, this coming in from the right, and shortly after, meet a gravel cycle track at a T-junction.

2. Turn left at the T-junction, ignore a grassy ride immediately to the left, and follow the gravel track as it goes sharply to the right. Skirt Busketts Lawn and Lodgehill Inclosures, eventually reach the grounds of Ironshill Lodge, and follow the cycle track as it goes sharply to the left at a T-junction.

   To take the shorter walk, turn right along the gravel track at this T-junction, and continue straight ahead to rejoin the main route a short distance before the start of Section 6. Note, however, that along here there is a crossing of Bartley Water to negotiate at a ford, which, particularly in winter and after heavy rain, can be too deep even for Wellington boots.

3. Otherwise, after going left at the T-junction, almost immediately go straight ahead at a crossroads, eventually turn very sharp right at another T-junction (cycle track sign number 44) and continue to follow the track through Lodgehill Inclosure and into Ironshill Inclosure.

4. Ignore a ride on the left and after a short distance, go downhill through the inclosure. Follow the track as it enters Busketts Lawn Inclosure, go straight ahead at a crossroads, and cross Bartley Water at a small bridge.

5. Follow the cycle track as it bears right, go straight ahead at another crossroads and eventually reach a T-junction – the left turn here, along the cycle track, leads to the parking spaces by the telephone box on Woodlands Road.

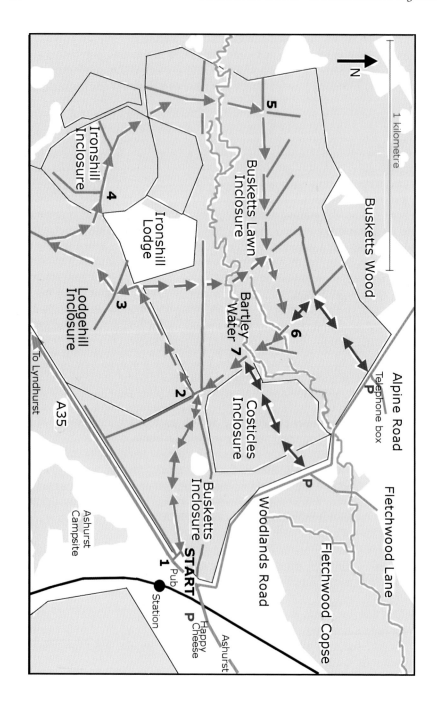

6. Otherwise, turn right along a well-made gravel track, pass a quite wide track coming in from the left, cross Bartley Water at a footbridge beside a much older ford, and reach another section of the cycle route at the next T-junction – the left turn here leads to the other Woodlands Road parking spaces.

7. Otherwise, continue straight ahead before eventually turning left immediately after passing a wide, woodland ride on the right, and just before the cycle track bears sharply right – this is the route used on the outward part of the walk. (Take care here to avoid the grassy ride that goes straight ahead on the cycle track bend).

   After a short distance, ignore a grassy ride on the left, continue straight ahead and reach the roadside stile by turning right when almost opposite The New Forest pub.

For the adventurous, for those with a good sense of direction, strong map reading skills and access to an Ordnance Survey map!
Create your own walk by combining parts of this route with elements of your choice from the following selection of connecting or conveniently located nearby routes.

From *New Forest Walks – a time traveller's guide*:
Walk 7   Ashurst: Churchplace Inclosure

From *New Forest Walks – a seasonal wildlife guide*:
Walk 4   Bartley Cricket
Walk 5   Ashurst: Churchplace Inclosure

Start	Small public car park beside the Happy Cheese pub, alongside the A35 in Ashurst - Ordnance Survey map reference SU335103. (Should space not be available here, alternative parking places can be found nearby)
Distance	5 kilometres (3 miles) Shorter walk: 3.5 kilometres (2 miles)
Time to allow	1¼ - 3 hours
Refreshments	The New Forest and the Happy Cheese are both close to the start of the walk
Route	Along readily visible tracks
Terrain	Mainly on level ground, but with a small number of gentle gradients
Rating	1 - easy walking
Buggies	Not suitable
Railway station	Ashurst (New Forest), adjacent to the start of the walk
Bus service	Bluestar
New Forest Tour Bus	Yes
Alternative start	None
Forest Holidays Caravan sites and campsites	Ashurst, 0.5 kilometres (⅓ mile)

Walk 7

Ashurst:
Churchplace Inclosure and Ashurst Wood

Setting the scene

Ashurst expanded significantly following the mid-19th century coming of the railway, but this walk avoids much of the village and instead goes through the primarily broadleaved woodlands of Churchplace Inclosure and Ashurst Wood.

The New Forest boundary, bordered by large, mossy wood-banks, is followed for part of the way alongside a disused medieval highway that itself took the probable route of a Roman road.

The keeper's cottage at the entrance to Churchplace Inclosure

Along the way

Ashurst (New Forest) railway station - more than a century and a half of service

Although now unmanned, this station on the London Waterloo to Weymouth main line has regular stopping trains. It also has a fascinating history. Opened as Lyndhurst Road station on June 1st 1847 – the day that the line carried its first passenger train – it was also referred to as Ashurst in some contemporary accounts. A horse drawn omnibus provided a link with Lyndhurst three times a day to meet the trains, and by 1904 a motor bus was operating on the route. A 1902 proposal, though, for an electric light railway was never implemented.

The station dealt with heavy timber traffic until 1964, and for many years, holiday makers had use of camping coaches, static railway coaches that were popular from the mid-1930s to the mid-1960s. A level crossing originally took the Lyndhurst road over the railway, but in 1932, with motor traffic increasing, the current bridge was built.

The adjacent pub, now known simply as The New Forest, was in 1898 the Railway Hotel, but by 1911 had become the New Forest Hotel. The station took its current name in June 1997.

Ashurst (New Forest) station

New Forest Union workhouse - a place of last resort

Charles Dickens in 1837 did much to cement the popular view of the workhouse when he put the immortal words 'Please sir, I want some more' into the youthful mouth of Oliver Twist. Often viewed as horrors of the Victorian age, workhouses did, however, provide the needy with useful help of last resort, and from the 1880s were not quite as bad as is often believed, although strictly laid down daily routines continued to be rigorously enforced and able-bodied residents were set to work for nine or ten hours each day.

Built in 1836 following the 1834 Poor Law Amendment Act, the New Forest Union workhouse was on the site of the present NHS Ashurst Centre, and provided accommodation for those with few alternatives: the sick, elderly, infirm, orphaned and poor of Beaulieu, Bramshaw, Dibden, Eling, Exbury with Lepe, Fawley, Lyndhurst and Minstead, and later, Colbury, Copythorne, Denny Lodge, East

Bramshaw, Marchwood and Netley Marsh.

The workhouse concept came to an end in 1930, and the building here was subsequently used as a Public Assistance Institution that continued to provide accommodation for those most in need. In the late 1940s, it was taken over by the fledgling National Health Service.

The old, ivy-clad red-brick building at the entrance to the site was the workhouse chapel, which probably dates from the third

The workhouse chapel

quarter of the 19th century – notice the Cross on the eastern gable end, and the bell, used to call residents to service, on the western end.

Churchplace Inclosure - boundary stones and the keeper's cottage

By the keeper's cottage, just beyond the right turn into Churchplace Inclosure, can be seen on the left in what appears to be an old pit - it's across a fence, just before a nearby gate - a round-topped, moss-encrusted stone marking

the New Forest boundary. It carries the date 1861 and the initials FP, maybe signifying Forest Perambulation. Other similar stones lie further on along the walk route, but they are now largely lost to sight under generations of leaf litter and other debris.

Notice, too, on the side of the cottage, a stone-carved fallow buck's head with the inscription 'J. Gulliver Keeper 1970'; whilst on the rear of the building, inset into the wall, is a tablet commemorating creation of the inclosure. On this, the area taken in is expressed in acres and the now oft-forgotten imperial units of roods and perches – A R P, 177 1 9¼. The name Glenbervie, also shown on the

The 1861 boundary stone

tablet, refers to Lord Glenbervie, Surveyor General of Woods and Forests at the time.

Churchplace Inclosure - the site of Ashurst Coppice

Churchplace Inclosure was first set aside for timber production in 1810, and some of the original oak and beech trees can still be seen. Conifers are present, too, although at least one large stand of mature Douglas firs was clear-felled in 2005, and the space planted with oak trees in 2007.

The inclosure was planted, though, partly on the site of an earlier block of woodland known as Ashers Coppice, or as it would now be called, Ashurst Coppice, which occupied the eastern end and, indeed, shared much of the same boundary. In 1575, there was documentary reference to a coppice 'new made' – almost certainly this – and in the late 18th century, Richardson, King and Driver's map continued to show it as New Coppice. Old, badly eroded 16th century boundary banks can still in places be seen.

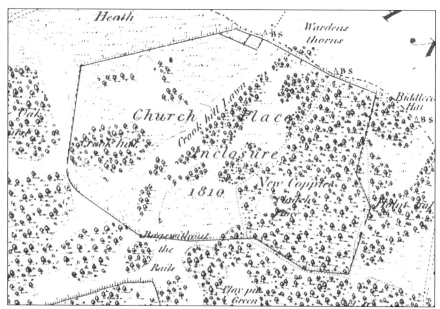

Churchplace Inclosure and New Coppice, as shown in 1814 by Richardson, King, Driver and Driver

Prior's Bushes, Wardens Thorns and a lost Roman road

Prior's Bushes, privately owned woodland adjacent to Churchplace Inclosure and the New Forest boundary, almost certainly takes its name from Breamore

Priory, a religious house lost during Henry VIII's 16th century dissolution of the monasteries, which until that time held Langley Manor, including the land on which this woodland is located.

Richardson, King and Driver's map, however, omits Prior's Bushes – the map was concerned mainly with New Forest lands – but marks the nearby position of Wardens Thorns on the boundary of land held then by the Wardens of Winchester College.

Today, substantial earthen banks border both the woodlands of Churchplace Inclosure and Prior's Bushes, leaving in-between what once was a well-used route, referred to in the 13th century as the King's Road, running along the likely line of a Roman road linking Applemore Hill with Cadnam, a Roman road that provided a convenient boundary for use when the New Forest was first created.

Part of the route taken by the 'King's Road', which ran along the likely line of a Roman road

Church Place – the site of a medieval keeper's lodge

Church Place is the modest hillock that gave its name to Churchplace Inclosure, but there is now no suggestion that a religious house once existed here, although in former times, this association was wrongly assigned to a number of unexplained earthworks in the mistaken belief that William the Conqueror destroyed whole villages, including their churches, to make way for his new hunting ground.

Church Place, the hillock, is now much overgrown

In fact, Church Place, along with The Churchyard, at Sloden, and Church Place, Denny, is the site of a medieval keeper's lodge dating from around the 14th century. Studley Castle, near Bramshaw Telegraph, is another lodge site; a fifth is close to Queen Bower, near Brockenhurst; whilst others are at Bolderwood and within the bounds of Lyndhurst Old Park.

Largely maintained into the 15th century, most of the lodges were relatively modest, timber framed dwellings constructed for use by Forest officials, including, latterly, woodmen; although the lodge at Bolderwood included a great chamber for the King's comfort, whilst another, New Lodge – thought to have been on the site of New Park, Brockenhurst – also had accommodation for royalty.

Here in Churchplace Inclosure, traces of the earthen bank that once surrounded the lodge can still be found, though now much obscured by vegetation.

Saltpetre House – a short-lived Elizabethan enterprise

To the south-west of Ashurst campsite, close to the road leading to Ashurst Lodge, can be found a series of irregular banks and hollows spread over a broadly rectangular 140 x 50 metres (460 x 165 feet) area, the remains of a Saltpetre House that from 1577 to 1584 manufactured this material for use in the production of gunpowder.

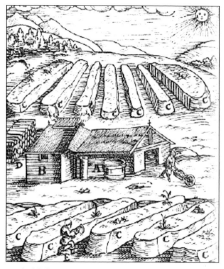

Until 1561, saltpetre was imported into Britain, but was subsequently produced using a mixture of urine, dung, lime and nitrogenous earth typically found in dovecotes and stables. Eventually, manufacture was undertaken using long rows of porous walled beds filled with vegetable waste, blood and dung, to which was added lime or ash. Underwood from Ashurst Wood may here have fuelled fires needed during the process, but use of timber was prohibited.

In 1604, 20 years after production ceased, the site was still sufficiently well-known to be used to denote part of the north-eastern extent of

A 16th century saltpetre plant illustrated in 'A collection of reproductions of Ancient Pictures Concerning the History of Gunpowder', published in 1906

the Manor of Lyndhurst. Coincidentally, the completely unrelated Salt Way, an ancient track used to transport salt inland from the nearby coastal salterns, passed a short distance to the north-west of the Saltpetre site.

The Route

If joining the route from the railway station, leave the station at the end of the platform serving trains going towards Brockenhurst and Christchurch, and walk along a fence-side tarmac path signed 'Way out to Ashurst Village'. Go through a gate and follow the path as it bends to the right, just before a railway bridge. Pass another gate, on the right; and reach the public car park – the walk start point.

1. Leave the car park on the side close to the Happy Cheese pub, pass a road on the right leading into the NHS Ashurst Centre – once the site of the New Forest Union workhouse – and follow the tarmac road running half-right, behind the Happy Cheese.

    After a short distance, go through a gate and continue straight ahead along a gravel track with fields on the left, and on the right, a small New Forest lawn that until relatively recently was used as a cricket pitch – on match days a sign was displayed asking walkers to wait for a break in the play before passing!

2. Pass a keeper's cottage on the right, turn right through an adjacent gate leading into Churchplace Inclosure, and absolutely immediately go left along a path leading into this attractive woodland.

3. After a short distance, where the main track goes half-right, uphill; follow a narrower path to the left, alongside a fence-line adjoining the adjacent, privately owned, primarily broadleaved woodland shown on the map as Prior's Bushes.

    Pass on the right an often flooded, overgrown pit, the site of old sand workings known locally as the Loom (loam) Pits. Follow the path alongside the fence past a further related area of diggings that are often obscured by bracken, and on until the end of the adjacent woodland is reached.

4. Here, as the fence goes right, turn even sharper right to follow a path running beside a block of conifers close to the edge of Deerleap Inclosure which, as it was not created until 1867, is one of the later New Forest inclosures.

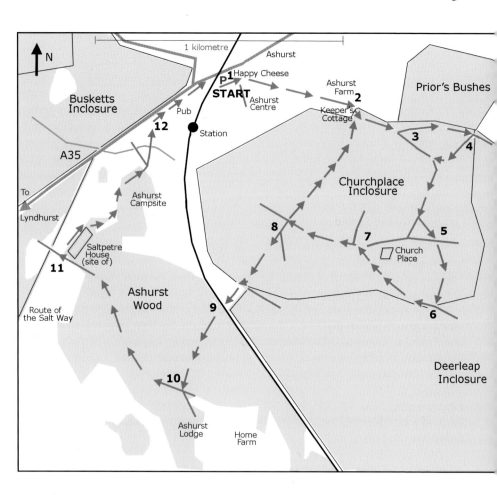

Reach a Y-junction adjacent to an area of relatively recently cleared conifers, and turn left beside a fence erected to prevent deer and commoners' stock from damaging the replacement stand of oaks. Then at the next Y-junction, take the left fork leading away from the fence-line.

5. Go straight ahead at an indistinct crossroad of tracks, carry on downhill through an area of conifers, and follow the path as it enters Deerleap Inclosure through a break in the boundary wood-bank.

6. Immediately turn right at a T-junction, and follow what here is a gravel cycle track, first downhill and then up a gentle gradient. The broadleaved woodland of Churchplace Inclosure is quickly re-entered – notice on the

left, running at a sharp angle to the cycle track, the substantial moss-encrusted earthen bank that again separates the two inclosures.

On the right along here is Church Place, a bracken-clad knoll topped with mature oak, beech and holly trees – the site of a medieval keeper's lodge.

7. Pass a turn on the right – this goes back alongside the area of clear-fell seen earlier – and continue along the cycle track as it bears left, downhill. Immediately miss a narrow path on the right, and eventually, at a T-junction of gravel tracks, turn left to follow the cycle track – ignore a grassy ride leading straight ahead here, which effectively makes this a crossroad of tracks.

   To take the shorter walk, turn right along the gravel track at this T-junction/crossroads, and continue straight ahead to reach the keeper's cottage passed earlier at the start of Section 2.

8. Otherwise, after a short distance, follow the path to the right at a Y-junction, with yet further to the right, another quite large area of clear-fell.

   Turn right at the next T-junction, where the path again meets a cycle track. Immediately go through a gate and follow the track as it bears to the left, across Crookhill Bridge leading over the railway line.

   The bridge was constructed in the year after the railway opened – visible from beside the fence adjoining the line, 1848 is marked on both sides of the bridge, together with W. & J. Lankester, Southampton, who, presumably, were the builders.

9. Continue straight ahead through Ashurst Wood, an area of magnificent ancient, unenclosed woodland where majestic oaks and beeches grow where nature, not man, intended; and reach on the left, the fenced grounds of Home Farm and the adjacent Ashurst Lodge.

   Ashurst Lodge was probably built in the 16th century to house the proprietor of the nearby Saltpetre House, one Cornelius Stephinsonn. It became the local underkeeper's residence, was used as a home for the elderly, and now is occupied by the Wessex Institute of Technology.

10. Go beside a low, Forestry Commission vehicle barrier and immediately turn right to follow a tarmac road running along a wooded ridge-way, past on the left a number of relatively recently pollarded mature hollies: trees with trunks cut off at head height to encourage new growths of dense, green foliage that will provide welcome forage for deer and commoners' stock.

    A short detour of around 75 metres to the left here leads to an area of glorious ancient beech woodland overlooking a wide expanse of grassland, heathland and scattered trees with, in the distance, the Beaulieu River at Longwater Lawn.

Continue along the tarmac road as it goes downhill beside, on the left, extensive open heath and grassland.

To the right here, shrouded in woodland, two impressively enormous parallel earthen banks set at right angles to the road enclose what once was a rectangular-shaped area used for the manufacture of Saltpetre.

11. Turn right immediately after (and beside) the saltpetre site to follow the woodland edge, and eventually emerge onto an area of grassland close to the Forest Holidays, Ashurst Campsite.

    Skirt the campsite, which was the location of a Second World War sawmill; cross a tarmac road leading towards the A35 campsite entrance; and continue half-left along a grassland path leading towards a roadside bus shelter.

    Cross a drainage channel at a small bridge, and go over a roadside stile.

12. Turn right alongside the A35 to follow the footpath past 'The New Forest' pub. Turn right beside the pub to return to the railway station. Alternatively, continue straight ahead, cross over the railway bridge, and the car park is on the right.

For the adventurous, for those with a good sense of direction, strong map reading skills and access to an Ordnance Survey map!

Create your own walk by combining parts of this route with elements of your choice from the following selection of connecting or conveniently located nearby routes.

From *New Forest Walks – a time traveller's guide*:
Walk 6   Ashurst: Busketts Inclosure

From *New Forest Walks – a seasonal wildlife guide*:
Walk 5   Ashurst: Churchplace Inclosure

Walk 8
Beaulieu Road: Black Down, Matley Holms, Matley Wood, Denny Wood and Shatterford

Cattle on the heath not far from the start of the walk

Setting the scene

Heathland; wide expanses of re-seeded grassland; narrow streams; quaking valley mires; aged hollies; broadleaved and coniferous inclosures; and ancient, unenclosed woodland: this walk has them all.

A section of the route follows the Cut Walk, an 18th century Master Keeper's road that for much of its course is now little more than a narrow track; and passes close to Beechen Lane, an early highway running between Lyndhurst and Denny Lodge.

Start	Shatterford, Forestry Commission car park, 5.5 kilometres (3½ miles) south-east of Lyndhurst on the B3056 Lyndhurst to Beaulieu road - Ordnance Survey map reference SU348064
Distance	9 kilometres (5½ miles)
Time to allow	2¼ - 5½ hours
Refreshments	The Drift Inn is close to the start of the walk
Route	In places, a little 'off the beaten track'
Terrain	Mainly on level ground, but with a small number of gentle gradients
Rating	2 - moderate walking
Buggies	Except after rain, the route in late spring and summer is usually suitable for sturdy buggies, although it is advisable to keep to the roadside verge during the short stretch alongside the B3056 Beaulieu Road (Section 6)
Railway station	Beaulieu Road, adjacent to the start of the walk
Bus service	None
New Forest Tour Bus	Yes
Alternative starts	1) Beaulieu Road, Forestry Commission car park, across the road from Beaulieu Road station - Ordnance Survey map reference SU351063 2) Matley, Forestry Commission car park, beside Matley Wood campsite, close to the route - Ordnance Survey map reference SU332073 3) From limited roadside parking beside the route near Denny Lodge - Ordnance Survey map reference SU334059
Forest Holidays Caravan sites and campsites	1) Matley Wood, on the route 2) Denny Wood, 1 kilometre (0.6 miles) north of the route

Along the way

Alder - coppices, pollards, gunpowder and gas masks

Many of the alder trees conspicuously present alongside the stream at King's Passage and Holmhill Passage – and elsewhere in the New Forest – show signs of past coppicing and pollarding, practices to which local alders were extensively subjected until at least the 1950s.

Coppiced alders at Holmhill Passage

But why was alder timber so extensively taken? Well, it resists decay in damp conditions and in early times was a much favoured material for making water pipes and wooden pumps. Alders were also used for foundation piles under bridges and houses, and during the 1940s, in Southampton docks. Before the widespread availability of conifers in the south of England, scaffolding, too, was constructed of straight-trunked alders.

The charcoal is also particularly suitable for use in the production of gunpowder, so there was considerable 19th century demand from the Fritham-based Schultze Gunpowder Factory; and it was ideal for the manufacture of First and Second World War gas mask filters.

Cut Walk - a master keeper's route across the Forest

Part of this walk route passes along a section of the Cut Walk, a centuries-old road that linked Lyndhurst, the New Forest's administrative and commercial centre, with the Marchwood home of the Master Keeper of East Bailiwick.

A sandy, heathland track and well-trodden way through Matley Wood, the Cut Walk was shown simply as *New Road* on the map

The route of the Cut Walk passes through Matley Wood

produced by Isaac Taylor in 1759, and then by its proper name on Richardson, King and Driver's late 18th century map.

A second road of similar vintage, also named the Cut Walk, was constructed to improve transport links between Lyndhurst and Burley Lodge, the home of successive Master Keepers of Burley Bailiwick.

Trench Mortar School and War Dog Training area - preparing for the Front

During much of the second half of the 19th century, and on into the early 20th century, the presence of wide open spaces and varied terrain, access to common land and the relative sparseness of the local population all encouraged use of the New Forest for military training, practice and manoeuvres. Indeed, much of the ground between Lyndhurst and Matley Wood, visited in part during this walk, was occupied by the military during the First World War.

The area immediately to the west of the wood, for example, was used as a trench mortar school, known locally as the Bombing, or Grenade, School. Trench mortars, relatively short-range artillery weapons, were new to the British Army at this time, so effective training was essential. Local disruption, although significant, was a price worth paying. Lyndhurst resident Charles Hall left a vivid description from 1916: 'The War was at its height and beyond

The Trench Mortar School site

Bolton's Bench in the distance was a bombing range where troops were trained in hand grenades (Mills bombs as they were called then) and land mines. No one was allowed beyond this hill, and there was an almost continuous sound of explosions and bangs coming from the range.'

An old photograph of the Bombing School class of 1916 shows seated in the front row, the son of Sir Arthur Conan Doyle. (Sir Arthur had a holiday home at nearby Minstead and is buried in the village churchyard.) Traces of the trench lines can still be seen, although the area was subsequently restored and partly ploughed. Large numbers of craters are also visible close to the alder carr in the north-west of the area – the pitted nature of the ground shows up well on Google Earth!

Nearby, the land around Matley Ridge was used for war dog training between 1917 and 1919 – from late in 1916, dogs were used by the British Army to carry messages from the front line, and for guard and sentry duty. These were not dogs familiar with the ways of the New Forest, however, as records from the time indicate a number of instances of cattle and pig worrying!

It is said that around 7,500 war dogs were killed in action.

Park Pale - an impressive, meandering earthwork

During this walk, the Park Pale is first encountered near Matley Ridge. An earthen bank with internal ditch, it once encircled what became known as Lyndhurst Old Park, a medieval deer park dating back to at least the 13th century. Development seems to have been in several phases, and even now the bank and ditch in places are enormous – with a paling fence on top, they would have presented an insurmountable obstacle for even the most energetic deer.

The Park Pale today encloses a flask-shaped area with a broad, open section running alongside Park Ground Inclosure, and a narrow neck situated between Beaulieu Road and the nearby Ridge. It has been suggested that deer were driven in at the open end, herded into the narrow neck and then shot; although recent research indicates that the original park was considerably larger than the area now enclosed, and was not flask-shaped at all.

A pony feeds in the ditch beside the Park Pale, illustrating the scale of this ancient boundary feature

By 1428, the park was reported to be poorly maintained, although disparking does not seem to have occurred until the 16th century. New Park, Brockenhurst, first noted in 1484, continued in use, however, and in 1670 was modified on the instructions of King Charles II to accommodate red deer newly brought over from France.

The Route

If travelling by train or using the Beaulieu Road car park, follow beside the B3056 as it crosses the railway bridge, and join the walk route where it leaves the Shatterford car park.

1. From the car park entrance, cross the minor road, turn right, and then left immediately before the railway bridge. Pass a low, Forestry Commission vehicle barrier, and follow the track that runs parallel to the railway line.

    Ignore a narrow, pedestrian bridge over the railway, and just beyond, go right at a fork in the track. Continue downhill for a short distance before taking a left-hand fork leading in the direction of a wide expanse of grassland that was cropped and re-seeded not long after the end of the Second World War.

2. Turn left and proceed in a clockwise direction until almost halfway round this grassland, all the time keeping close to its edge; then turn left again along a pronounced track leading towards King's Passage, a passing place over a very wet area of alder carr flanking a narrow tributary of the Beaulieu River.

    Tradition has it that this place was so-named after King Charles II in the 17th century crossed the stream here, probably whilst out hunting.

3. Cross two small bridges and a causeway – not in this sequence – constructed to take the track through the wetland area, and immediately after the second bridge, fork left around the edge of another post-Second World War cropped and re-seeded lawn. Go up a slight incline, and at the top, go half-left along a grassy track leading towards Matley Wood.

4. Reach a T-junction – despite a narrow, animal pathway opposite, this can hardly be described as a crossroads – and turn left along a quite wide, sandy track (the old Cut Walk) leading into Matley Wood.

    After a short distance, follow the more pronounced right-hand fork in the track, and eventually meet a low, Forestry Commission vehicle barrier at the edge of Matley Wood campsite.

5. Immediately beyond the barrier, continue straight ahead along a gravel track
    – this is actually a right turn at a T-junction, but effectively, the track goes
    straight ahead. Ignore other tracks on the left leading into the campsite, and
    continue along the main track as it skirts Matley Heath on the right.

    *Across the heath to the right, up on a distant hill overlooking Lyndhurst,
    is the pale outline of Northerwood House where King George III was a guest
    in 1789 - for a number of years after, to mark the event, the house was
    known as Mount Royal. Nearby is the tall spire of Lyndhurst's 19th century
    parish church, whilst the Trench Mortar School was further still to the right,
    alongside the western edge of Matley Wood.*

    Leave the campsite, and immediately cross the B3056 and an adjacent
    narrow strip of heath at Matley Ridge.

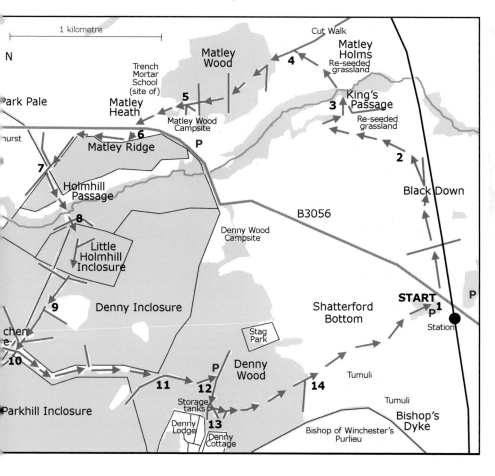

6. Turn right to follow the coniferous woodland edge, initially passing over a series of bumps and undulations, the remains of past gravel diggings. Ignore two quite wide tracks leading into the conifers, and immediately after the second track, follow the woodland edge to the left.

   Continue down a gentle incline, ignore a track coming in from the right, and pass through a gap in the still impressive earthen bank that is the Park Pale.

7. Almost immediately, turn left along a track leading downhill through the trees of Denny Inclosure. Cross Holmhill Passage – a narrow strip of boggy ground – and go over a stream at a bridge, the same stream encountered earlier, and as before, flanked here by alder carr.

   Notice the deep-banked, relatively straight, somewhat artificial appearance of the watercourse; whilst upstream, close to the left-hand bank, is an often wet meander cut off from the main flow. Both are sure signs of past management designed to reduce flooding by speeding the river's passage.

8. After a short distance, go through a gate and walk uphill through the broadleaved woodland of Little Holmhill Inclosure. Pass a track on the left in the midst of the wood, and eventually leave the broadleaves as Denny Inclosure is re-entered.

   Continue straight ahead with, after a short distance, conifers on both sides, and on the left beyond the trees, an area of re-growing clear-fell.

9. Pass a track on the left and after 300 metres, go through a gate with gravel track beyond.

   Straight ahead is a cycle track through Parkhill Inclosure, whilst to the right is Beechen Lane, a track marked on Isaac Taylor's 1759 map as Beeches Lane, and the main route from Lyndhurst to Denny Lodge. It was recorded as the King's highway in the 14th century, and may have been used by the Cistercian monks of Beaulieu. The possibility of Roman origin has also been suggested.

10. After going through the gate, turn left to follow a narrow path running close to the Denny Inclosure fence. At first the path follows along the edge of a narrow strip of heathland before fence and path bear left, eventually passing through a belt of ancient, unenclosed woodland separating Denny and Parkhill Inclosures.

    Ignore a gate on the left, and continue along the driftway before more fully entering the ancient, unenclosed woodland of Denny Wood. *Notice on the left along here, a number of small, old pits, overgrown in summer by bracken, and bordered by wonderfully moss-encrusted banks.*

11. Just beyond the end of the left-hand inclosure fence-line, turn left along a gravel track.

12. Eventually pass beside a low, Forestry Commission vehicle barrier, and turn right immediately after, along a tarmac road with a sign intended for vehicles, reading 'Access to Private Properties Only'.

13. Reach the top of a short hill, and when opposite two storage tanks set into the ground on the right, follow a quite wide, grassy track to the left into the wood.

    Almost immediately reach a junction of tracks, and continue half-to-the-left through the trees, ignoring the track going downhill to the right. Soon after, ignore another fairly indistinct path coming in from the right, and follow the track as it continues to bear half-left, eventually downhill towards a wide expanse of open heath and bog beyond the wood.

    A little to the north of the route here, is the site of an old Stag Park similar in age to that within Highland Water Inclosure – mentioned during Walk 4.

14. Go straight ahead over the heath, heading in the direction of a row of distant, pale-coloured cottages and a clump of pines around the Shatterford car park. *Mid-way along here, from the slightly higher ground close to Shatterford Bottom, notice to the right on the near horizon the low, rounded mound of a bracken-covered Bronze Age barrow, and beyond, to the left, the outline of two more barrows.*

    Cross the causeway over Shatterford Bottom, and the car park is up ahead, with the railway station beyond.

For the adventurous, for those with a good sense of direction, strong map reading skills and access to an Ordnance Survey map!
Create your own walk by combining parts of this route with elements of your choice from the following selection of connecting or conveniently located nearby routes.

From *New Forest Walks – a time traveller's guide*:
Walk 9   Beaulieu Road: Shatterford

From *New Forest Walks – a seasonal wildlife guide*:
Walk 6   Beaulieu Road: Shatterford
Walk 9   Lyndhurst: Clay Hill

Start	Shatterford, Forestry Commission car park, 5.5 kilometres (3½ miles) south-east of Lyndhurst on the B3056 Lyndhurst to Beaulieu road - Ordnance Survey map reference SU348064
Distance	4.5 kilometres (2¾ miles)
Time to allow	1 - 2¾ hours
Refreshments	The Drift Inn is close to the start of the walk
Route	Along readily visible tracks
Terrain	Mainly on level ground, but with a small number of gentle gradients
Rating	1 - easy walking
Buggies	Except after rain, the route in late spring and summer is usually suitable for sturdy buggies. However, tree roots sprawl across the path in Denny Wood, and the return track in places is over sandy ground
Railway station	Beaulieu Road, adjacent to the start of the walk
Bus service	None
New Forest Tour Bus	Yes
Alternative start	Beaulieu Road, Forestry Commission car park, across the road from Beaulieu Road station - Ordnance Survey map reference SU351063
Forest Holidays Caravan sites and campsites	1) Matley Wood, 2.5 kilometres (1½ miles) 2) Denny Wood, 2 kilometres (1¼ miles)

Walk 9
Beaulieu Road:
Shatterford, Bishop's Dyke,
Denny Wood and Woodfidley

A colourful sunset over Shatterford Bottom

Setting the scene

This relatively short walk on level ground crosses a wide expanse of heathland before passing through the edge of ancient, unenclosed woodland. For a while, the route follows Bishop's Dyke, a medieval earthwork enclosing the Bishop of Winchester's Purlieu.

Woodfidley, halfway round, was the site of a woodland inclosure created in 1700, but subsumed one hundred-sixty years later within the considerably larger Denny Lodge Inclosure. Woodfidley rain, an old, now rarely heard, local saying, refers to rain that lasts all day.

Along the way

Bronze Age barrows - last resting places

The Bronze Age began in Britain after the probable introduction from mainland Europe of bronze tools, weapons and related manufacturing techniques, and lasted from around 2000 BC until 650 BC, after which, as iron-making knowledge increased, bronze was gradually superseded as the metal of choice. The new ways spread slowly at first, but the impact on relatively primitive men previously reliant on stone and bone, revolutionised the way people lived and worked.

Bronze Age barrows – ancient burial mounds, the last resting places of tribal leaders and other prominent members of society – are abundantly present in

A prominent Bronze Age barrow on nearby Yew Tree Heath

the New Forest, and are shown on Ordnance Survey maps as *Tumuli* (the plural) or *Tumulus* (the singular). Shaped like upturned earthen pudding basins, many of the barrows were known as butts, for they were apparently often used as archery butts during target practice.

Typically dating back to the early/middle Bronze Age – around 3,500-4,000 years ago – the barrows were created as the final act of an ancient funerary rite. A sacred, circular area set aside for burials would usually be surrounded by an earthen bank and ditch, and a causeway created to give access to the interior. Cremation of human remains was common practice, and the ashes of the deceased, placed in a pottery vessel, would be buried in a freshly dug pit within the circle, which would sometimes be used over several years for further interments. When no longer needed, the circle would be sealed with a large mound of earth, the remains of which are what we see today.

Six barrows are visible during this walk, whilst around 250 remain in total. Virtually all are of a type known as bowl barrows; most have been badly eroded by the weather, trampled by commoners' stock and damaged by rabbits; and many, too, have been horribly mutilated, often centuries ago, by amateur antiquarians, treasure hunters, and the curious, people who often clumsily dug down into the mounds with little attempt at subsequent restoration and without publishing relevant details of their results. Recorded finds have, however, included burnt earth, wood reduced by fire to charcoal, and coarse urns containing ashes and burnt bones.

Most of the barrows are now protected by law as Scheduled Ancient Monuments that are not to be walked or ridden across or in any way damaged. Indeed, the Forestry Commission a number of years ago announced that special protection measures for some would be put in place.

Heathland - a man-made landscape
Have you ever wondered about the origin of heathland, such as that encountered during this walk? Maybe not, but there's a simple explanation for its formation, an explanation that dates back in many places to the Bronze Age, and maybe earlier, when men cleared woodland on poor soils, repeatedly used the land for agriculture – which caused the loss of further nutrients – and in the process, created ground able to support acid-tolerant heathland vegetation, but not much else.

In time, however, many of the heaths would have naturally reverted to woodland if it had not been for exploitation by man. Gorse, for example, provided feed in-situ for domestic animals, cutting and chopping made it even more palatable, charcoal burners took their share, and so did people wanting fuel for firing ovens and kilns. Turves, also, were cut for the fires; and bracken was used extensively for bedding and litter. Heather, too, provided bedding material, and was used as thatch and as an underlying layer below many gravel tracks.

Outside the New Forest, many former heathlands have been lost to cultivation; are under tarmac, bricks and concrete; or through neglect, have simply gone back to woodland. Here, too, without the presence of commoners' stock and effective management – periodic, deliberately started fires; and individual removal of stubborn saplings – invading pine and birch would re-start the process of woodland development, taking from future generations the opportunity to experience heathland landscapes and wildlife.

Heather grows well in impoverished, acidic soil

Bishop's Dyke - an ancient earthwork

The earthen bank and ditch of Bishop's Dyke winds a 7.25 kilometres (4½ miles) serpentine course, and encloses 202 hectares (500 acres) of low-lying, boggy ground. Up to 4 metres (13 feet) wide and 1 metre (3¼ feet) high, it is also known as the Bishop's Ditch, and the enclosed land, the Bishop of Winchester's Purlieu – a purlieu is land once within the jurisdiction of the Forest, but no longer so.

Heywood Sumner, writing in 1923, tells that the earthwork originated in the 13th century when in 1284, John de Pontoise, Bishop of Winchester, obtained the grant of Bishop's Ditch from King Edward I. The extent of land included was said to be all that the Bishop could crawl round in a day on his hands and knees,

Bishop's Dyke, here topped with heathers, crosses the landscape

although Sumner rightly dismissed this story, saying: 'The legend – which occurs elsewhere – seems to express country humour, attributing a fantastic origin to an unusual earthwork of which nothing is known.'

Recent research by local historian Richard Reeves has, however, revealed that the land within Bishop's Dyke, known then as Penimore, was granted in 1213 to Peter des Roches, Bishop of Winchester. Authority to enclose it with a deer-proof bank and ditch – the one seen today – was given in 1216. Initially, the land was probably used as a deer park – the Bishop was known to be an enthusiast of the chase – but by 1244 it was in use as the medieval equivalent of a cattle farm.

Penny Moor on modern maps is shown beside the railway that now intersects the purlieu.

The land was returned to the Crown in 1944.

Charcoal making – a traditional New Forest industry

Charcoal has a long history of production in the New Forest; and at Woodfidley some of the evidence can still be seen – the remains of an old, particularly prominent, circular charcoal burners' pit with broad surrounding earthen bank part-obscured by short-cropped grass and bracken, one of at least three located quite close together here.

New Forest charcoal burners at work in Mark Ash Wood featured in an 1848 edition of the Illustrated London News

Yes, this is an old trade that dates back locally to at least Roman times, a trade that remained little changed until the early years of the 20th century. Simply put, a stack of small wood overlain by soil and turves was burnt over a period of several days in a repeatedly used pit; draughts were carefully controlled to produce a long, smouldering burn; and as constant attention was needed, the charcoal makers stayed on-site for the duration of the process, living in primitive huts constructed of branches, turf, bracken and whatever else came to hand.

Charcoal burning in the New Forest was, though, viewed by the Crown as an evil that detracted from the production of timber, and in 1698 restrictions were imposed on the trade. Success seems to have been limited, however, for a 1789 report noted that twenty-six coal hearths, or charcoal pits, were operating, many in defiance of the 1698 regulations.

Applications for the finished product were many. Charcoal burns at a high temperature, for example, which made it particularly suitable for use during metal smelting operations. Blacksmiths also used large quantities for their fires; it was a constituent of gunpowder; and a popular domestic fuel. Eventually, though, coke was to progressively come into general use as a superior alternative for many industrial purposes, whilst the railways made available low cost coal.

By the late 19th century, the charcoal burners had largely disappeared from these woods, although production did resume on a limited basis during the First World War, when charcoal was used, for example, in the manufacture of gas mask filters, and has continued intermittently ever since. From the 1920s, however, the traditional wood stacks and charcoal pits have been replaced by portable iron containers.

The 1851 Deer Removal Act, the third Act of Parliament to authorise creation of timber plantations

Deer can often be seen in the New Forest, sometimes right the way through the day, yet from at least the late 18th century, proposals were periodically made for the removal of absolutely all these graceful creatures, proposals that with the coming of the 1851 Deer Removal Act led to the extermination of most of those present – 3,000, or so, fallow deer, and up to 100 red deer.

But what had the deer done to deserve such a fate? Well, they competed with the commoners' stock for food. Deer management and damage caused was costly to the Crown. And unless well-fenced out, they wandered onto adjacent private land, much to the annoyance of the owners.

The 1851 Act was, however, also concerned with increasing the Crown's interests in the New Forest, whilst reducing the value and extent of common

The sight and sound of rutting fallow deer largely became a thing of the past

rights; thereby maximising the likely allocation of land to the Crown following any future disafforestation. And so provision was included in the Act for the compilation of a full register of common rights; and for the creation of further woodland inclosures from which commoners' stock, as always, would initially be excluded, these inclosures, disingenuously, in compensation for loss of the deer, even though the deer had been of little benefit to the Crown for a great many years.

Anyway, within the allotted time period of two years, most of the deer were shot, netted or otherwise removed, although it proved impossible to deal with every last one. The register of common rights was eventually compiled, and the Crown took up with enthusiasm its new planting rights, in the process taking in much valuable common land including, in 1860, that for Denny Lodge Inclosure, passed on this walk.

Postscript to the 1851 Act - and things eventually got better

The Act failed to please a great many people, and, in particular, the commoners. The register of rights was less generous in its allocations than had been anticipated; and following removal of the deer, the useful pasturage available for stock actually decreased as the deer had previously prevented the spread onto the lawns of rough, often inedible vegetation.

Furthermore, the speed and extent of new inclosure creation heightened fears that all the best land would eventually be taken for silviculture. Marginal land, too, was increasingly threatened as, for the first time, the Act permitted the extensive use of conifers, fast

The creation of many new coniferous inclosures followed authorisation by the 1851 Act

growing, commercially valuable trees that are less demanding of soil conditions than the broadleaved crops previously intended for use as navy timber. (Until then, relatively limited numbers of conifers had been grown, primarily to provide shelter for oak saplings in exposed situations).

Following the Act, conifers, somewhat predictably, were planted in large numbers in many of the new inclosures, and later, also as frequent replacements for both felled conifers and broadleaves, with an inevitable, detrimental impact on the landscape that continues to this day. Even the general public, many of whom were travelling in as visitors on the relatively newly opened railways, were quick to voice concerns.

Grievances were considered by an 1868 select committee of the House of Lords which concluded, despite opposition from local people fearful of the impact on commoning, that disafforestation was the best way forward. In 1871, a Bill to this effect was presented to Parliament, but later withdrawn; and then in 1875 a further select committee found in favour of both commoning and amenity issues, saving the New Forest as we know it and leading to the 1877 New Forest Act.

Often referred to as 'the Commoners' Charter', the 1877 Act was the first amenity legislation in the New Forest. Amongst other things, further enclosure was restricted to areas that had already been enclosed using powers granted by previous New Forest Acts, a provision that held until 1949 after which, with the agreement of the Verderers, a small number of additional inclosures were made.

And even the deer returned, slowly at first, but return they did.

(To provide timber in support of the First and Second World War efforts, many of the conifers planted following the 1851 Act (and some oaks) were felled. Replacements were often, though, further conifers).

The Route

If travelling by train or using the Beaulieu Road car park, follow beside the B3056 as it crosses the railway bridge, and turn left along the gravel track into the Shatterford car park.

1. Leave the car park by walking to the far end of the adjacent group of pine trees, and then walk along the wide part-grass, part-gravel track leading diagonally across the heath towards Denny Wood.

    Cross a gravelled causeway and bridge at Shatterford Bottom. *Beyond, where the ground levels out after a gentle incline, notice back to the left on the near horizon the rounded mounds of two quite large, Bronze Age barrows.*

    Barrows such as these were often placed in prominent positions. Both here can be seen from much of the walk route, although the right-hand one, topped with bracken, is particularly visible. Away to their right, further bracken-shrouded barrows lie closer to the path – the first obscures sight of the second and a more modestly sized third.

    Just before the wood is reached, take the first left-hand fork in the track, and 30-40 metres further on, follow the path to the left alongside a small group of silver birch trees.

2. Enter the ancient, unenclosed woodlands of Denny Wood. Turn left downhill at the next T-junction and continue parallel to the woodland/heathland edge – a little care is needed along here as the path is quite uneven.

    A short detour to the left immediately before entering the wood provides a panoramic view over an area of low-lying land, with the earthen bank of Bishop's Dyke prominently visible as it snakes over this ancient landscape.

    Follow the path downhill and after a short distance, on the left can again be seen Bishop's Dyke running alongside the woodland edge. Continue here along the now quite indistinct path within the wood.

3. Go left at the next T-junction, heading towards a footbridge over a narrow drainage channel.

    Cross over this bridge, and immediately afterwards another un-railed bridge. Follow the path half-left across the heath; and after crossing the next bridge, continue straight ahead and cross a further bridge some 300 metres distant. Continue on as the path again bends half-left, crosses a small un-railed bridge, and goes into a group of trees.

4. Immediately pass a track on the left and go up a gentle incline as the path runs parallel to the wood-bank and fence-line of Denny Lodge Inclosure. Continue on, out of these trees, heading towards another group of trees close to Woodfidley Passage.

   Pass a patch of heather straddling both sides of the path, and a narrow band of bracken. Look out then for a narrow, animal track on the left at the start of the next patch of heather – around 2/3 of the way between the two groups of trees – for this leads to the charcoal burners' pit, which is to the left of a lone hawthorn 20 metres from the main track.

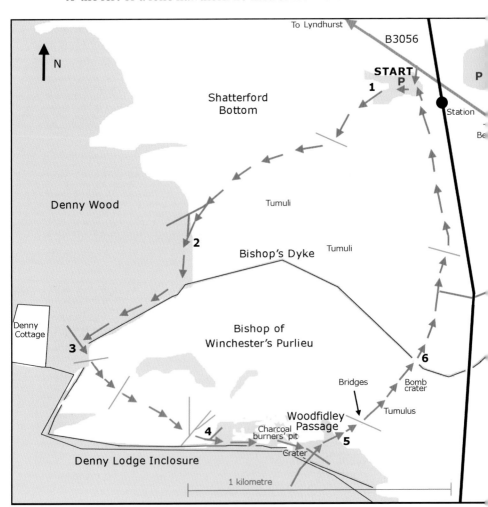

Return to the main track and after a short distance pass a substantial crater on the right.

This dates back to the Second World War and was created by an enormous parachute mine, probably destined for Southampton. These devices and their method of delivery were designed to cause maximum surface damage, but as the parachutes tended to drift in the wind, they sometimes landed a long way from their intended target.

Immediately after the crater, turn left at a crossroads to pass through the Woodfidley Passage group of trees.

5. Continue straight ahead over the heath, crossing in quick succession two bridges over narrow streams.

   Another Bronze Age barrow stands beside the track on the right here, not far beyond the second bridge; half-to-the-left, outlined against the skyline, are the two barrows seen earlier; and a little further on, to the right of the track, is another large, Second World War bomb crater recently exposed to view following Forestry Commission burning of the surrounding gorse and heather.

6. Pass through a gap in Bishop's Dyke and continue along the sand and gravel track. Ignore a turn on the right leading towards a railway bridge where small, disused, often water-filled sand and gravel pits provide a useful resource for wildlife and commoners' stock in need of a drink.
   Go over a gravelled causeway, and the car park and station are straight ahead.

For the adventurous, for those with a good sense of direction, strong map reading skills and access to an Ordnance Survey map!
Create your own walk by combining parts of this route with elements of your choice from the following selection of connecting or conveniently located nearby routes.

From *New Forest Walks – a time traveller's guide*:
Walk 8   Beaulieu Road: Black Down
Walk 11   Brockenhurst: Balmer Lawn

From *New Forest Walks – a seasonal wildlife guide*:
Walk 6   Beaulieu Road: Shatterford

Start	Hawkhill Forestry Commission car park, 0.75 kilometres (½ mile) east of Stockley Cottage on the B3055 Brockenhurst to Beaulieu road - Ordnance Survey map reference SU351019. (Note: the car park sign is not readily visible from the road)
Distance	9 kilometres (5½ miles) Shorter walk: 7 kilometres (4¼ miles)
Time to allow	2¼ - 5½ hours
Refreshments	Montagu Arms Hotel, Beaulieu - 4.25 kilometres (2¾ miles); Turfcutters Arms, East Boldre - 3.5 kilometres (2 miles)
Route	Along readily visible tracks
Terrain	Mainly on level ground, although parts of the route are along tracks surfaced with concrete that has in places broken up, so take care not to trip
Rating	2 - moderate walking
Buggies	Not suitable
Railway station	Brockenhurst, 5.75 kilometres (3½ miles)
Bus service	Wilts and Dorset serve nearby Hatchet Pond, primarily on Tuesdays, Thursdays and Saturdays only
New Forest Tour Bus	Yes, if the route is joined from the Beaulieu Heath, Forestry Commission car park
Alternative starts	1) Stockley, Forestry Commission car park, close to Stockley Cottage at Ordnance Survey map reference SU343018 2) Roundhill campsite 3) Beaulieu Heath, Forestry Commission car park, near the Model Aircraft Flying Area at Ordnance Survey map reference SU358006
Forest Holidays Caravan sites and campsites	1) Roundhill, on the route 2) Hollands Wood, 6 kilometres (3¾ miles)

Walk 10

Beaulieu Heath's Second World War airfield

Setting the scene

The wide open spaces of heather, gorse and wetland south-west of Beaulieu are home to an astonishing variety of wildlife, and on all but the dullest days provide tantalising views of the Isle of Wight's hump-backed hills. Yet this ancient New Forest landscape has for many years been more associated with aircraft than anything else. In fact, the connection goes back almost to the first days of powered flight, for in 1910 one of Britain's first flying schools was established at East Boldre on a site used in the First World War for Royal Flying Corps pilot training, and known from 1918 until closure in 1919 as RAF Beaulieu.

This walk, however, is centred on nearby sections of Beaulieu Heath where in 1940 work began on the construction of a much larger Second World War airfield. After starting on the edge of Hawkhill Inclosure, the route continues

Ponies by the edge of one of the main runways

along disused service roads and taxi-tracks, past old runways along which roared monsters of the sky. Fading outlines remind of long-gone workshops and hangars, whilst a number of other, more complete structures continue to defy the ravages of time. All have tales to tell of yesteryear's heroic deeds, and although none has tremendous architectural merit, their relationship with times of unprecedented national danger contributes to a somewhat humbling experience for visitors.

Along the way

Beaulieu Airfield - a significant contribution to the war effort

One of eleven Second World War airfields located in and around the New Forest, the one on Beaulieu Heath became operational in August 1942, initially as a base for Coastal Command long-range bombers such as the Liberator and Halifax. The crews' remit was straightforward, but the task much less so: patrol the eastern Atlantic and prevent U-boat attacks on convoys moving troops from Britain and the USA to fight in the North African Campaign. Commemorated in a panel set into the concrete close to the eastern end

Squadron Leader David Mackie Sleep, DFC, is remembered in a panel set into the concrete close to the eastern end of the main runway

of the main runway, Squadron Leader David Mackie Sleep, DFC, in October 1942 was the first Beaulieu-based pilot to sink a U-boat. His ashes, fittingly, were scattered on the airfield following his death in June 1989.

Early in 1944, after Allied victory in North Africa, the Coastal Command aircraft made way for fighter-bombers brought in prior to Operation Overlord, the invasion of mainland Europe that began with the 6th June, D-Day Normandy Landings. Typhoons flown by the RAF and the Royal New Zealand Airforce, assisted for a short time by Boston light-bombers, initially attacked targets in northern France in preparation for the later full-scale assault; whilst from early March to late June, USAAF P-47 Thunderbolts took over the work and went on to support the invasion. B-26 Marauder medium bombers subsequently used the airfield until September 1944 whilst providing aerial back-up for troops moving inland from the beachheads and continuing on through France and into Germany.

From late 1944 until September 1950, the Airborne Forces Experimental Establishment (AFEE) were present, testing gliders, glider tugs, helicopters and parachute equipment, and undertaking very limited pilot training; after which, although never called into action, the airfield was repaired and retained until 1957 as a US Airforce stand-by site.

Runways, taxi-tracks and aircraft dispersal pans

Still clearly visible as a series of wide, ghostly, grassy corridors, the airfield's three runways were set out in the shape of an enormous letter 'A' so as to provide take-off and landing facilities whatever the wind direction. The original concrete skimmed with tarmac was almost wholly removed in the 1990s for use in road construction projects although in places narrow strips can still be seen. The sole remaining substantial length, together with an adjacent area of concrete set down in the early 1950s during the airfield's 'stand-by' years, is currently used for flying model aircraft.

Heathers encroach onto one of the old, now grassy runways

Aligned east-west to take advantage of the prevailing winds, the main runway – the cross-piece of the 'A' – was bordered on both sides by lights, and so, to a lesser extent, were the subsidiary runways; but except for occasional concrete surrounds, none survives.

The surrounding taxi-track, now far narrower than in war-time, is used in part as a cycle track.

Evidence of dispersal pans, places around the perimeter of the airfield set aside for standing aircraft, has largely disappeared, but scattered gravel and occasional concrete fragments hint at former use, whilst close to the start of Section 10 of the walk, two building bases and much dispersal pan concrete remain.

Accommodation, hangars and workshops

In the area now largely taken by Roundhill campsite, bumps, hollows, bricks, concrete, an old water tower and four ivy-clad huts betray the location of the airfield's main accommodation quarters. Members of the Women's Auxiliary Air Force (WAAF) were billeted a little to the south where today brick and concrete building bases and two old air raid shelters stand incongruously on the edge of a field. (Other similar shelters around the airfield were removed many years ago).

An air raid shelter on one of the WAAF accommodation sites

Passed quite early in the walk, a large expanse of concrete marks the site of a hangar latterly used by AFEE 'B' Flight to house Sikorsky R4 and R6 helicopters; whilst across the adjacent service road were workshops, and buildings used by AFEE 'C' Flight, the Paratroop Section responsible for testing parachutes, associated planes and equipment. Here, narrow concrete and once-gravelled paths remain, and so do wider, now grassy access roads and an inconspicuous patch of concrete and gravel half-hidden by encroaching vegetation.

AFEE 'A' Flight, users of Horsar gliders capable of carrying 28-30 men or a jeep and gun; and Hamilcar gliders that could transport a tank, had hangar space close to the southern section of the taxi-track.

Bomb storage and airfield defence

First planted in 1870, Hawkhill Inclosure was used as a bomb storage site, and the service road leading to the airfield as a means of transporting the deadly cargoes.

Evidence amongst the trees of wartime usage is not difficult to find. Go through the gate at the northern end of the car park, for example, enter the woodland, proceed along the right-hand track, and on the right after a short distance is a concrete base, the remains of a long-forgotten small pyrotechnics store where Berry Pistol cartridges were held

A lone pony in the mist watches over the bomb storage site

that when fired, produced flares used for signaling aircraft; and smoke generators used by AFEE 'C' Flight to establish extent and direction of wind drift. Then continue straight ahead, go over the first crossroads, and after the concrete track bends left into a clearing, another building base or hard-standing can be found on the right, close to a long, low, brick wall, a bomb loading platform that has at one end what appears to be a small concrete shelter.

Army personnel present to defend the airfield were based a little to the west, on the edge of Stockley Inclosure, where a quite extensive complex of brick and concrete building bases engulfed in moss and leaves lies clustered beneath original planting 1809 oaks.

The Route

1. Leave the car park along the entrance road, and go straight across the nearby minor road – the B3055 running between Brockenhurst and Beaulieu.

    A Bronze Age barrow is by the roadside immediately to the right here, its low, broad mound topped with grass, heather and gorse. Numerous others occur elsewhere on the heath, although examination of old maps suggests that no less than seven were destroyed during construction and operation of the airfield.

    Follow the cycle track south along the old service road leading from the bomb storage site to the airfield.

2. Turn right at the next T-junction; follow the cycle track along the tarmac surfaced, disused taxi-track; and as it goes round to the left, pass on the left the end of one of the runways.

3. Eventually, just after the tarmac gives way for a short distance to compacted gravel, follow the cycle track as it goes sharply right – be sure here to ignore the quite substantial track leading straight ahead.

    On the left close to this turn, a shallow, gravelled, often water-filled hollow marks the site of the airfield control tower.

    After a short distance, pass on the right, the quite large concrete-surfaced site of the AFEE 'B' Flight hangar; whilst just beyond, on the left of the cycle track, is the rounded hillock of another Bronze Age barrow.

    Pass on the left immediately after the barrow, a narrow concrete-surfaced path that led to the airfield workshops and the AFEE 'C' Flight parachute packing facility.

    After a further 100 metres, turn left at a T-junction to continue along a branch of the cycle track that was originally a service road linking the airfield with the accommodation quarters.

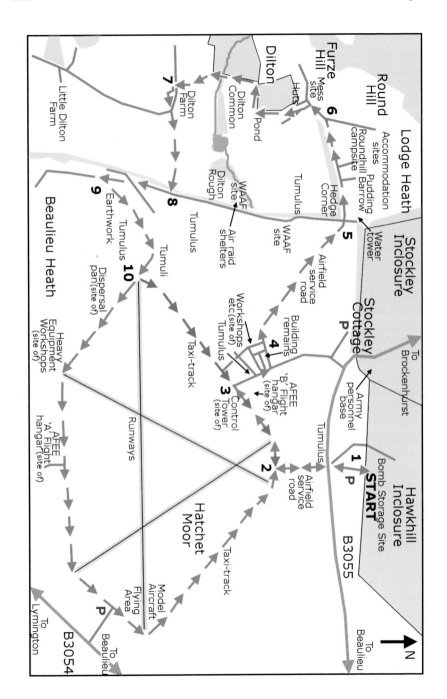

4. After a short distance, ignore another concrete-surfaced turning on the left, and continue along the cycle track as it first goes right, and then continues straight ahead.

5. Reach the more wooded landscape close to Hedge Corner, and pass beside a low, Forestry Commission vehicle barrier on the edge of Roundhill campsite.

    Notice to the right, half-hidden amongst a group of trees, the old water tower previously mentioned; and to the right of the track leading to the tower, a series of bumps and hollows, and a concrete base. Concrete and brickwork set into the grass is also visible nearby, whilst straight ahead of the barrier, surrounded by a wire fence, is a substantial Bronze Age barrow appropriately known as Pudding Barrow.

    Immediately after the vehicle barrier, ignore on the left a grassy track leading to the WAAF accommodation sites, and instead follow a narrow tarmac road going half-to-the-left beside the campsite. Ignore minor tracks on the right, and after 0.5 kilometres (¹/₃ mile), pass beside another low, Forestry Commission vehicle barrier.

    The field on the left along here was used by airfield personnel as a football and rugby pitch. When it was returned to the farmer in around 1949, the games took place beside the main runway, albeit interrupted by incoming and outgoing aircraft!

6. Leave the cycle track where it turns sharply right, and go left beside another low, Forestry Commission vehicle barrier to follow a broken concrete-surfaced road.

    After a short distance, as this road continues to the right, turn left through the left-most of two farm gates and follow a bridleway that almost immediately goes sharply right and then left before continuing as a narrow path bordered by brambles, bracken and gorse.

    To the right here are four dilapidated, asbestos-roofed, ivy and moss-clad buildings, Handcraft huts once used to accommodate airmen and other personnel.

    Pass an overgrown pond on the left, and follow the path as it immediately goes right and eventually left, uphill for a short distance. Cross a narrow valley with alder carr and a small stream in the bottom, eventually pass on the left a large barn associated with Dilton Farm, and go through an adjacent gate.

7. Ignore the left turn immediately alongside the barn as this leads into the farmyard, but take the adjacent left turn and go through another gate.

Follow here a narrow bridleway as it first goes right and then left around the edge of two old corrugated metal barns, abandoned Nissen huts acquired from the authorities and moved here, or maybe used for accommodation by outlying airfield personnel.

Immediately pass a more recent barn; cross a compacted dirt track leading on the left to the farm, and used as a bridleway to the right; and continue straight ahead, following another bridleway sign, through a gate and into a field.

Turn left and then right to follow the field-edge fence-line, go through a gate (or cross the adjacent, poorly maintained stile) and continue alongside the fence before passing through another gate to reach the edge of Beaulieu Heath.

At the edge of the field, around 400 metres to the left, are the two WAAF air raid shelters and brick and concrete building bases mentioned earlier; whilst by the gate, a substantial earthen bank with fence atop marks the New Forest boundary. Beyond is a parallel, less substantial bank with in-between, a quite marked, in places somewhat raised, 15 metres wide linear feature. Known to pre-date 1254, origin as a Roman estate boundary has been suggested.

8. Cross this tree-clad boundary feature and immediately after, turn right along a quite wide grassy ride bordered on both sides by gorse. Eventually go straight ahead at a four-way junction of tracks and continue for around 300 metres, ignoring along the way a number of minor tracks on the left.

9. At the next Y-junction, turn sharply left to follow what here is a fairly substantial dirt track running back across the heath.

   Visible on the left along here, 250-350 metres away, is a large, gorse-clad Bronze Age barrow. Other, much smaller, barrows can also be seen on the left, close to the next right-hand bend in the track.

10. Soon after this bend, rejoin the old taxi-track.

    To take the shorter walk, turn left here, continue straight ahead, eventually pass a grassy/gravel track on the left, and soon after rejoin the outward route at Section 3.

    Otherwise, turn right to follow the taxi-track past the sites of a prominent dispersal pan, the Heavy Equipment Workshops and the AFEE 'A' Flight hangar. Go through the Beaulieu Heath, Forestry Commission car park, pass beside the Model Aircraft Flying Area and continue along the taxi-track to rejoin the outward route at Section 2. (Be sure to ignore the right turn out of the car park, as this leads to the B3054 Beaulieu to Lymington road; and after that, if in doubt, follow the cycle track signs).

In recent years, a notice attached to a simple wooden post placed beside the Model Aircraft Flying Area replicated one overlooking the wartime airfield at Tangmere. It read:

> *"Today it is 'a peaceful scene under an English heaven', but as you look, remember the many thousands of men and women who worked, fought and sometimes died here, whose efforts helped ensure the peace and freedom we take for granted today. Let them not be carelessly forgotten".*

A Remembrance Day Cross and poppy, also attached to the post, added poignancy to the words and reminded again of the sacrifices made by many of the people once stationed here.

For the adventurous, for those with a good sense of direction, strong map reading skills and access to an Ordnance Survey map!

Create your own walk by combining parts of this route with elements of your choice from the following selection of connecting or conveniently located nearby routes.

From *New Forest Walks – a seasonal wildlife guide*:
Walk 7   Crockford Bridge, Beaulieu Heath

Start	Tilery Road, Forestry Commission car park, 1.5 kilometres (1 mile) north-east of Brockenhurst village centre, off the B3055 Brockenhurst to Beaulieu road - Ordnance Survey map reference SU308033
Distance	8 kilometres (5 miles) Shorter walk: 2 kilometres (1¼ miles)
Time to allow	2 - 5 hours
Refreshments	The Snakecatcher, the Rose and Crown and the Foresters Arms are all in Brockenhurst village
Route	Along readily visible tracks
Terrain	Mainly on level ground, but with a small number of gentle gradients
Rating	2 - moderate walking
Buggies	Not suitable
Railway station	Brockenhurst, 1.75 kilometres (1 mile)
Bus service	Bluestar and National Express
New Forest Tour Bus	Yes
Alternative starts	1) Standing Hat, Forestry Commission car park, on the route at Ordnance Survey map reference SU314036 2) Balmer Lawn, Forestry Commission car park - beside the river, close to the Balmer Lawn Hotel - Ordnance Survey map reference SU303031
Forest Holidays Caravan sites and campsites	1) Hollands Wood, 0.5 kilometres (⅓ mile) 2) Aldridge Hill, 4 kilometres (2½ miles)

Walk 11

Brockenhurst: Balmer Lawn; Parkhill, Stubby Copse and Ramnor Inclosures

The track leading to Standing Hat

Setting the scene

Starting a little to the north-east of Brockenhurst, this walk passes by the extensive, hummock-strewn grasslands of Balmer Lawn before meandering through a number of 18th and 19th century woodland inclosures – Pignal Inclosure dates back to 1751, Stubby Copse and Ramnor to around 1829, Pignalhill to around 1846, and Parkhill to 1853.

Along the way

Brusher Mills - the New Forest's Victorian snake catcher

Visitors to Brockenhurst might wonder about the name of the Snakecatcher pub, situated on the main A337, close to the railway level crossing. Once

A youthful-looking Brusher Mills poses for the camera, complete with snakes and snake catching paraphernalia

known as the Railway Inn, the change of name was in honour of Harry 'Brusher' Mills, a regular customer and renowned New Forest snake catcher.

Born in 1840 in a cottage at Emery Down, near Lyndhurst, Brusher worked for a while as a labourer at nearby Clayhill, but by 1880, apparently prompted by Lord Londesborough of Northerwood House, Emery Down, he had embarked on the career that was to assure a place in New Forest folklore. Adders, grass snakes and smooth snakes were all caught and stored in a dustbin, many awaiting despatch to the London Zoological Society where they were fed live to king cobras and other large snakes.

His nickname was said to derive from a habit of brushing the cricket pitch at Balmer Lawn, or from brushing the ice for skaters on a local lake. He lived for many years in a charcoal burner's abandoned hut, but in 1903 unseen hands, maybe afraid that overlong occupation would confer rights of ownership, destroyed this humble dwelling, and thereby evicted the old man.

Local folklore has it that Brusher died with heart and spirit broken, which may, in part, be true, for he passed away in July, 1905 whilst at the Railway Inn – the cause of death: heart disease. He was buried in Brockenhurst parish churchyard where his ornate headstone can still be seen.

Balmer Lawn - a change of name and mysterious mounds

Balmer Lawn, an extensive area of grassland at the start of this walk, was until the 19th century known as Palmers, or Palmer, Lawn; whilst the nearby Lymington River was Palmers Water, and so was an adjacent hamlet. But the exact identity of Palmer remains a mystery, for this is an old Brockenhurst family name going back to at least the 14th century, and nobody knows for sure after which Palmer these places were named.

Although at times the lawn can still be very wet, it was extensively drained in the mid-19th century and acts as a magnet for commoners' stock attracted by the rich grazing. It was the site of a golf course and of regular pony races, but perhaps the most noticeable feature today is the multitude of low, closely packed mounds once thought to be intensely grazed purple moor grass tussocks that assumed their current form following drainage. Recent

The landscape of low, closely packed mounds on Balmer Lawn

research, however, suggests that they were made by hoards of yellow meadow ants that colonised the drying land, but then largely abandoned the sites as the drains progressively lost effectiveness and the ground again became wetter.

Balmer Lawn Hotel - a hospital and war-time planning base

Overlooking the Balmer Lawn grasslands, the Balmer Lawn Hotel is an impressive reminder of the days of grand, country houses. Built at the beginning of the 20th century, it is on the site of an earlier bungalow used as a pub called The Holt, which presumably reflected the presence of otters in the nearby river.

Located conveniently close to the south coast, the hotel was used during the First World War as a field hospital, initially attached to the Lady Hardinge Hospital for wounded Indian soldiers evacuated to Britain from the battle zones, and later attached to the No. 1 New Zealand General Hospital. The bodies of more than one hundred military personnel who did not survive are buried in the 'New Zealand cemetery' in Brockenhurst parish churchyard, whilst nearby

The Balmer Lawn Hotel was used as a field hospital during the First World War

Meerut Road recalls the presence of soldiers from the Meerut Division of the Indian Army.

Used first as an Army Staff College during the Second World War, the hotel subsequently saw service as a base for planning the Normandy invasion.

Victoria Brick and Tile Works - an enterprise initially funded by the railway

The Tilery Road car park takes its name from the Victoria Brick and Tile Works, located a little to the north-east, which operated from the mid-19th century until the first quarter of the 20th century. Built by Josiah Parkes, a leading drainage expert, the works manufactured tile-pipes used underground to drain water and deposit it into often specially cut, open ditches that today still crisscross much of the New Forest.

Woodland bumps and hollows betray the location of the old clay pit north-west of Standing Hat

Initial funds for the enterprise were available, at least in part, from the Southampton and Dorchester Railway Company which in 1845 made a substantial compensation payment associated with access to their route across the Forest – the money was specifically set aside for the joint benefit of Crown and commoners in draining the Forest.

Victoria Tilery Cottage – the manager's bungalow, converted to a house – still stands, and evidence of associated clay extraction can be seen, including, visible from the walk route, a deep, disused pit. Clay was also extracted from another similar pit, passed on the shorter version of this walk, a little to the north-west of the Standing Hat car park. Nothing of the factory remains.

The Frohawk Ride - butterflies galore

The Frohawk Ride, a bramble-lined path mid-way through this walk, was designated in 1995 by the Forestry Commission to commemorate Frederick William Frohawk (1861-1946), who was a frequent visitor to the New Forest. An eminent naturalist perhaps best known for his outstanding contribution to butterfly studies, Frohawk was also a writer and accomplished wildlife artist who produced and illustrated the highly regarded *Natural History of British Butterflies* and other titles. Indeed, Frohawk was so enthusiastic about

Magnificent silver-washed fritillary butterflies can still be seen along the Frohawk Ride

butterflies that he named his daughter Valezina after a particularly attractive female form of the silver-washed fritillary.

Today, these woods still harbour silver-washed fritillaries, including the Valezina variant; and also strong populations of the rare, pearl-bordered fritillary; white admirals; brimstones; speckled woods; ringlets and many more.

The Route

From Brockenhurst village centre and the railway station

Leave the village centre on the main A337, heading north towards Lyndhurst. When 1 kilometre (0.6 miles) from the railway level crossing, go over the river at a road bridge and immediately after, turn right into Balmer Lawn Road, the B3055 signposted to Beaulieu and Roundhill Campsite. The Balmer Lawn Hotel can be seen to the left, whilst the Balmer Lawn, Forestry Commission car park is beside the river on the right.

After 400 metres, where the road bends to the right, follow a wide, gravel Forestry Commission track leading straight ahead towards the distant woods. The Tilery Road car park is a short distance ahead on the left.

1. **From Tilery Road car park**

   Turn left out of the Tilery Road car park to continue along the gravel track leading towards the distant woods. Cross over a bridge; pass on the right a small area of grassland with clumps of gorse, bordered by broadleaved trees; and pass on the left, ancient, unenclosed woodland. Go left at a fork in the track, following the directions on a sign advising: 'All Cyclists, Walkers and Vehicles this way'.

   Standing Hat, with its own small car park, is on the left.

2. **To take the shorter walk, go across the Standing Hat car park and follow the path beside the fence-line past the bumps and hollows of an old clay pit until a gate is reached on the right. Turn left here to follow the remainder of the route from the start of Section 10.**

   Otherwise, before entering the wood, turn right opposite the car park entrance; pass a low, Forestry Commission vehicle barrier; and follow the gravel cycle track for a short distance as it passes behind a cluster of buildings associated with Victoria Tilery Cottage.

3. Continue straight ahead where the cycle track bends to the right, and go along a quite wide, grassy ride between two inclosures.

   Follow this driftway around to the left, ignoring almost immediately a gated track on the right. Pass another gate and track on the left, cross a narrow stream – Etherise Gutter – at a bridge, and turn left at a T-junction beside a small stock pound, to go along a narrow, gravel cycle track.

4. Continue straight ahead along the driftway where almost immediately the cycle track goes left. Cross a drainage channel, eventually pass a gate on the right, and start to climb gently uphill.

   Cross another gravel cycle track and follow the driftway downhill, now between Stubby Copse Inclosure on the right and Parkhill Inclosure on the left. Cross a drainage channel at a bridge, pass a gate on the left, and another on the right.

5. Where the driftway disappears, giving way to a narrow band of ancient, unenclosed woodland, turn left through a pedestrian gate and take the narrow, grassy path into what here is the primarily coniferous woodland of Parkhill Inclosure.

   Almost immediately take the left fork at a Y-junction, and continue along this quite wide, grassy ride.

   Go straight ahead at a crossroad of grassy rides, turn right at the next

T-junction, meet a junction of gravel cycle tracks, and directly opposite is a Forestry Commission sign and interpretation board introducing the Frohawk Ride.

6. Go along this wide, grassy ride; cross a drainage channel; and eventually, at the end of the ride, go straight ahead at a crossroad of tracks to follow a gravel cycle track. At the next T-junction, where the cycle track bears left, go straight ahead along a continuation of the original gravel track.

7. At the next crossroad of tracks, notice the enormous ornamental conifers on both sides, and oak woodland recently thinned to provide space to grow for the trees that remain. Turn left here along another grassy ride, leading

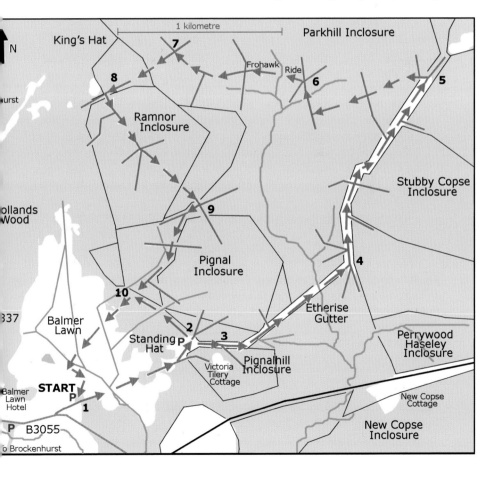

towards a gate out of the inclosure.

The path continues through the gate where, in marked contrast to the inclosure, ancient, unenclosed woodland is now present on both sides. A short distance away to the left is the Ramnor Inclosure fence and beyond, well-spaced, mature, inclosure oaks.

8. Continue up a gentle incline and at the top, turn left through a gate leading into Ramnor Inclosure. Meet a cycle track at a T-junction, and continue straight ahead.

    After a short distance, at a junction of five tracks, cross a gravel cycle track and continue straight ahead along a grassy ride that eventually goes gently downhill to meet a crossroads.

9. Turn right here, along the cycle track and then almost immediately, as the track starts to go downhill, turn left along a grassy ride beside Pignal Inclosure. Go straight ahead at a crossroad of grassy rides, and pass another grassy ride on the left.

10. Go through a gate and enter a section of ancient, unenclosed woodland bordering Balmer Lawn – a section of woodland left uncut when the inclosures were created.

    Continue straight ahead out of the wood and over the lawn. After a short distance, use a small bridge to cross a drainage channel and again go straight ahead, following a quite wide path where the old mounds have been trodden flat.

    Cross another two bridges, turn left immediately after the second to follow beside a drainage channel, and then turn right to reach the nearby Tilery Road car park where a metal water trough is visible on the edge of the trees.

For the adventurous, for those with a good sense of direction, strong map reading skills and access to an Ordnance Survey map!

Create your own walk by combining parts of this route with elements of your choice from the following selection of connecting or conveniently located nearby routes.

From *New Forest Walks – a time traveller's guide*:
Walk 9   Beaulieu Road: Shatterford

From *New Forest Walks – a seasonal wildlife guide*:
Walk 8   Brockenhurst: Balmer Lawn
Walk 9   Lyndhurst: Clay Hill

Walk 12
Brockenhurst: Black Knowl, Ober Water, Ober Heath, Poundhill Heath, Queens Meadow and Highland Water

Autumnal colours near Ober Corner

Setting the scene

Readily accessible by train and local bus services, the start of this walk is also quite close to the route of the New Forest Tour Bus, which operates in the summer months.

Ober Water is the first of three streams encountered along the way, followed by Fletchers Water and Highland Water. Ancient, unenclosed woodlands at Ober Corner and around the historic Queen Bower are on the route, and so are a number of 19th century broadleaved and coniferous woodland inclosures.

Along the way

Black Knowl and the New Forest's re-seeded lawns - the needs of wartime

Black Knowl is one of a number of former heathland and acid grassland sites set down to lawn following, in most cases, arable cropping designed to combat

Start	A track leading from Meerut Road to the village allotments, 1 kilometre (0.6 miles) north of Brockenhurst village centre - Ordnance Survey map reference SU299028. Note: parking is not available beside this track
Distance	7.25 kilometres (4½ miles) Shorter walk: 3 kilometres (1¾ miles)
Time to allow	1¾ - 4½ hours
Refreshments	The Snakecatcher, the Rose and Crown and the Foresters Arms are all in Brockenhurst village
Route	Along readily visible tracks
Terrain	Mainly on level ground, but with a small number of gentle gradients
Rating	2 - moderate walking
Buggies	Except after rain, the route in late spring and summer is usually suitable for sturdy buggies, although in places the ground can be a little bumpy
Railway station	Brockenhurst, 1.5 kilometres (1 mile)
Bus service	Bluestar and National Express
New Forest Tour Bus	Yes
Alternative starts	1) Public car park in Brockenhurst village centre, close to the Post Office in Brookley Road at Ordnance Survey map reference SU298023 - this is not shown on the sketch map 2) Balmer Lawn, Forestry Commission car park beside the river, close to the Balmer Lawn Hotel, 1 kilometre (0.6 mile) from the start of the walk - Ordnance Survey map reference SU303031 3) Ober Corner, Forestry Commission car park, on the route at Ordnance Survey map reference SU284036

Alternative starts (cont'd)	4) Beachern Wood, Forestry Commission car park, close to the route on Rhinefield Road at Ordnance Survey map reference SU284027
Forest Holidays Caravan sites and campsites	1) Aldridge Hill, on the route. 2) Hollands Wood, 1.5 kilometres (1 mile) from the start of the walk

Second World War-related food shortages. Much of the western section here, however, was too wet to support crops, so drainage was improved using ridge-and-furrow ploughing, and the land immediately re-seeded. (Undulating evidence of the ploughing can still be seen, particularly to the left of the path used after passing the allotments).

The new lawns improved the extent and quality of grazing for commoners' stock, although now, after more than 50 years, nature is exerting an increasingly strong influence, and in places, heather has reappeared amongst the close-cropped grasses and low-growing plants that have adapted to survive the grazing pressure.

Black Knowl, with Water Copse Inclosure beyond

Fletchers Water and Highland Water - 19th century 'improvements'

Fletchers Water joins Highland Water at Queen Bower, and is crossed during this walk on the edge of Ober Heath. But despite its natural appearance, the course of the stream here is of man-made origin, cut straight and true to reduce flooding and

thereby improve grazing and timber growing conditions. The original course can still be seen, particularly after wet weather, on both sides of the Ober Heath path, 100 metres (328 feet), or so, before the stream.

Highland Water, encountered a little later in the walk route, was also subject to 19th century 'improvement' – the main flow was diverted from its course across Queens Meadow and

Fletchers Water in high summer

through what is now adjacent wet woodland, to follow the current channel alongside the south-western edge of the Meadow. The remains of the old, badly silted stream can be seen where it re-joins the new 'cut' close to Queen Bower.

Queens Meadow, Queen Meadow Leys and Queen Bower - royalty remembered

This walk takes in Queens Meadow, a broadly square area of open grassland; passes close to the site of Queen Meadow Leys, a one-time meadow that now is wooded; goes through the ancient, unenclosed woodlands of Queen Bower; and skirts the site of a medieval keeper's lodge.

All have long histories. Meadow, Leys and Bower are shown in the late 18th century on Richardson, King and Driver's map, whilst documentary reference to the lodge, referred to as *Queneboure*, dates back to 1428 when even then it was in ruins – it is known that a number of New Forest lodges were constructed following a 1358 order of Edward III.

But which queen lent her title to this delightful part of the New Forest? Well, repairs to a mill *with accommodation for the Queen*, situated close to nearby Bolderford Bridge, were recorded in 1310. Perhaps, then, the queen in question

The Queen Bower lodge site - part of the substantial earthen bank with adjoining ditch

was Isabella of France, who married Edward II in 1308; or Margaret of France, second wife of Edward I from 1299 until his death in 1307.

Local historian Richard Reeves, though, convincingly puts the case for Eleanor of Castile, wife of Edward I from 1254 to 1290 – it seems likely that a queen stayed at the mill some time significantly before 1310, as the building was then already in need of what are thought to have been substantial repairs; it is known that Eleanor acquired and increased her interests in the New Forest from 1266 until her death; and that she also, according to tradition, made Lyndhurst her home whilst Edward was away fighting the French.

Today, the lodge site comprises a substantial earthen bank with adjoining, sometimes water-filled, ditch which perhaps served as a defensive moat. West Country slate, the remains of roofing material, has been found at the site, which was cut in two in the 1850s by the modified course of Fletchers Water.

Hydraulic Ram - a tribute to Victorian ingenuity

Elements of a mid-19th century hydraulic ram system are present close to Bolderford Bridge. A mechanically simple system, without any other external source of power, it pumped water from the river up to a storage tank in the grounds of nearby New Park – a short detour to the left immediately before the bridge provides views over to New Park Farm and the flat-roofed building on which the tank was situated.

Evidence of the hydraulic ram system remains by the trackside

Across the bridge, right beside the track is an associated square, brick chamber straddling a narrow, often dry water channel; whilst further along the channel is a dilapidated, roofless building housing part of the pump mechanism.

Based on a late 18th century invention, systems such as this were widely used in rural areas, and in many places continue to be of value.

The Route

From Brockenhurst village centre, the railway station and public car park

From the main A337 adjacent to the railway station entrance, facing north on the Lyndhurst side of the level crossing, turn first left along Brookley Road. After 300 metres, go straight ahead at a crossroads where Brookley Road is intersected by the B3055, Sway Road. Pass through the main shopping area – the public car park is on the right here, almost opposite the Post Office. Use the pedestrian bridge to cross the Watersplash – where the road crosses a ford – and turn right along Burley Road.

After 250 metres, pass Brookside Road on the right; take the next right turn down Meerut Road; and continue on beside the grasslands of Butts Lawn on the left. The entrance to the allotments, and the start of the walk, is 400 metres ahead, on the left not far before the Cloud Hotel.

From the Balmer Lawn, Forestry Commission car park beside the river, close to the Balmer Lawn Hotel

Turn left out of the car park, go left again along the footpath beside the main A337, and cross the road bridge over the river.

Notice on the left just beyond the bridge, an old, grey roadside milestone associated with the Lymington, Lyndhurst and Rumbridge Turnpike Trust, 1765, which used this route – the stone gives Lymington as V (5) miles and Lyndhurst III (3) miles.

After another 275 metres, turn right into Meerut Road. The entrance to the allotments is 450 metres ahead, on the right not far beyond the Cloud Hotel – ignore along here Martin's Road on the right, two turns on the left for Waters Green, and a further turn on the left called Butts Lawn.

1. Start the walk by turning off Meerut Road and going along a gravel track leading towards the village allotments and Black Knowl, an extensive area of

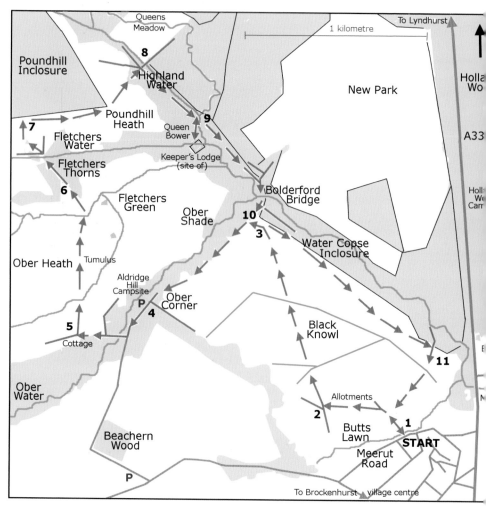

open grassland interspersed with gorse, birch and occasional pines.

Beside the road, cross a bridge over a small stream; then immediately before the gate leading into the allotments, go left parallel to the allotments fence and pass through an area that once was also allotment grounds.

2. At the end of the fence-line, turn right along a narrow gravel track and continue diagonally across Black Knowl until the woodland of Water Copse Inclosure – dating back to around 1829 – is almost reached.

3. **To take the shorter walk, turn right here and follow the remainder of the route from the start of Section 10.**
Otherwise turn half-left, and join a well-made, gravel cycle track.

4. Pass on the right the Ober Corner car park, and continue straight ahead for a short distance along a tarmac road through ancient, unenclosed woodland. Turn right along a gravel road at the sign for Aldridge Hill campsite, and cross Ober Water at a bridge. Pass a turn on the right leading to the campsite, and go on towards the white-washed, keeper's cottage.

5. Immediately after the cottage, turn right beside a narrow drainage channel, skirt a small group of trees on the right, cross another drainage channel at a low bridge, and join a path running straight ahead across the flat, heathery expanse of Ober Heath.
Mid-way across the heath, a Bronze Age barrow lies to the right of the path; whilst to the left can be glimpsed in the distance through a gap in the trees, the roof and chimneys of Rhinefield House. Built between 1888-92 on the site of a New Forest keeper's lodge, this is now a hotel.
As the path bends left, cross a bridge over a stream and then pass on the left a deer observation platform half-concealed amongst Scots pine foliage.

6. Leave Ober Heath through a narrow band of woodland – Fletchers Thorns. Cross Fletchers Water at a bridge; immediately after, turn half-left to pass through an area of hawthorns and blackthorns; and then go straight across the narrow neck of Poundhill Heath.

7. Turn right to follow the edge of Poundhill Inclosure, first planted in 1859, and pass another deer observation platform on the edge of the wood. Mature conifers quickly give way to a more recent planting, whilst at the end of the fence-line is a sign advising: 'Wildlife Conservation Area, Please Avoid Disturbance, All Dogs on leads, please'.

Cross a narrow drainage channel and follow the path as it goes slightly left across open heathland, heading for a patch of broadleaved woodland skirted by pioneering birch trees.

8. Cross a bridge over Highland Water to obtain views over Queens Meadow from a nearby gate. This a favourite place of fallow and sometimes red deer. It is also part of the Wildlife Conservation Area, entry to the field is prohibited and dogs should still be kept on leads.

   Retrace the route back across the bridge, and follow the river to the left as it flows downstream, through beautiful ancient, unenclosed woodland, towards Queen Bower.

9. Reach another bridge over the river, and immediately before crossing, detour to the right to follow the stream for a short distance.

   Around 50-75 metres to the right of this streamside path are a number of shallow, disused clay pits and the remains of three roughly circular, temporary clamp kilns used, it has been suggested, to make bricks for the 17th century construction of nearby Hursthill Lodge – now demolished – and possibly buildings at New Park.

   Further along this path, intersected by the mid-19th century cut of Fletchers Water, are the wasted earthwork remains of the Queen Bower medieval keeper's lodge.

   Retrace the route back to the bridge, cross over the stream and leave the Wildlife Conservation Area. Follow the path as it goes left, then right – around an area of damp ground – and then goes straight ahead alongside an inclosure fence on the left.

   Meet a T-junction, turn right along a gravel track, cross the river at Bolderford Bridge, and continue straight ahead for a short distance – the remains of the hydraulic ram system are on the left here. Immediately after, pass a path on the left leading through Water Copse Inclosure.

10. Immediately after that, turn left to follow a strip of grassland running close to the edge of Black Knowl a short distance from, and parallel to, the woodland edge.

11. When almost at the far end of Black Knowl, just after the inclosure wood-bank is met on the left, take the path to the right, through the gorse – this is opposite a pronounced track on the left, going through a glade of aged hollies.

   Cross a water channel at a small bridge, continue straight ahead to reach the track leading to the allotments, and retrace your steps to the start of the walk.

Walk 13

Burley New, Burley Old, Dames Slough, Anderwood and Burley Outer Rails Inclosures

Setting the scene

Two and a quarter kilometres (1½ miles) north-east of Burley village centre, the Lucy Hill car park is an ideal starting point for rambles in the surrounding woodlands. Gravel tracks and two short stretches of minor road are used during this walk, which is suitable for young children in sturdy buggies.

After leaving the car park, one of the minor roads is followed for a short distance, bordered on the left by ancient, unenclosed woodlands; and on the right by Burley New Inclosure where, despite the name, the first trees were planted way back in 1810. Burley Old Inclosure puts the 'new' into context, however, for this was created in 1700, although many of the original trees have been felled and replaced with more recent plantings. Dames Slough Inclosure (around 1860) is met with next, and then comes Anderwood (1811), before the circuit is completed in Burley Outer Rails Inclosure (1810).

Glorious ancient, unenclosed woodland close to Lyndhurst Road at the start of the walk

Start	Lucy Hill, Forestry Commission car park on Lyndhurst Road - Ordnance Survey map reference SU227045
Distance	8.5 kilometres (5¼ miles)
Time to allow	2 - 5¼ hours
Refreshments	The Queens Head and the Burley Inn are both in Burley village
Route	Along readily visible gravel tracks and two short sections of road
Terrain	Mainly on level ground, but with a small number of gentle gradients
Rating	2 - moderate walking
Buggies	Suitable for sturdy buggies
Railway station	Sway, 12 kilometres (7½ miles)
Bus service	Wilts and Dorset serve nearby Burley village, primarily on Mondays, Wednesdays and Fridays only
New Forest Tour Bus	Serves nearby Burley village
Alternative starts	1) Oakley, Forestry Commission car park, across the road from Lucy Hill - Ordnance Survey map reference SU226046 2) Anderwood, Forestry Commission car park, on the route 1.5 kilometres (1 mile) west of the A35, close to Anderwood Cottage at Ordnance Survey map reference SU249058
Forest Holidays Caravan sites and campsites	1) Holmsley, 8.5 kilometres (5¼ miles) 2) Setthorns, 10.75 kilometres (6¾ miles)

Along the way

Common of Mast - of pigs and pannage

Look out for autumnal, free-ranging pigs during this and other New Forest woodland walks. Now somewhat out-of-keeping with much of the modern world, pigs were once an important part of the rural economy. Indeed, Domesday Book in 1086 noted for many areas of woodland, the number of pigs that could be supported; whilst until relatively recent times, cottage families would often keep a pig and feed well through winter on the salted pork.

This New Forest sow, lying on a bed of bracken, wears a contented expression as her piglets suckle

But in the New Forest, pigs continue to be put out by local people who occupy land to which is attached the right known as *common of mast* – the animals fatten on a diet of fallen acorns and beech mast, which is good for the pigs and also good for ponies and cattle, for acorns are poisonous to ponies and cattle, but not to pigs.

Pigs can occasionally be seen at other times of year, but it is during the autumnal *pannage season* that most appear. Lasting for a minimum of 60 days, the start of the season is determined by the weather and when the acorns fall, and is agreed between the Forestry Commission and the New Forest Verderers. If the crop is particularly heavy or if few pigs have been put out, an extension may be authorised. The number put out depends largely upon the strength of the acorn crop and, to some extent, potential financial returns. In recent years, numbers have varied between 300 and 575.

Cockroad Hill - an old name and a bit of mystery, too

Cockroad Hill, on the southern edge of Burley New Inclosure, is shown on Richardson, King and Driver's late

A frosty morning at Red Rise, adjacent to Cockroad Lawn

Burley Outer Rails Inclosure took part of Burley Lodge grounds

18th century map, along with nearby Cockroad Lawn, another Cock Road Hill and a Cock Road. There is also a reference to the *Cocke Rode* – as it was spelt – in a 1604 Manor of Lyndhurst boundary schedule.

These, then, are old names, but how have they arisen? Well, some suggest that they refer to the presence of woodcocks, for from at least the 13th to the 19th centuries these rotund, long-billed game birds were trapped in fine mesh nets erected in favoured woodland glades, and the routes along which they flew were known as *cockroads*. Indeed, the birds' spring-time display flight is still known as *roding*. Other people, though, say that *Cock Road* is a medieval term for the King's highway, although no such route is known to have passed this way.

Burley Lodge - tales of wealth and privilege

Situated 3.5 kilometres (2 miles) to the north-east of Burley village centre, Burley Lodge was first mentioned in contemporary documents in 1490; whilst from 1690, Charles Paulet, who was to become the 2nd Duke of Bolton, held Burley Bailiwick and lived at the lodge, as did successive members of the family until the early 19th century.

In 1791, however, William Gilpin, Vicar of Boldre, seemed singularly unimpressed when noting that the property made 'an excellent Forest lodge, but a poor ducal seat', and continued: 'The late Duke' (presumably the 5th Duke, who passed away in 1765) 'was at some expense in adorning it. He built handsome stables, fitted up the house and laid up a lawn before it, which is bounded by a piece of embanked water. There is but little taste however, shown in the improvement.........'

The 6th Duke died in 1794, without a male heir, and the dukedom became extinct. In 1809 the Crown purchased the outstanding portion of the lease from the Dowager Duchess, after which the main house was demolished and a substantial part of the grounds were taken for Burley Outer Rails Inclosure. A second, smaller lodge was constructed on the site, or an earlier building retained, for use by New Forest keepers and subsequently as a farmhouse.

Perhaps not surprisingly, the Dukes of Bolton left other reminders of their presence. Bolton's Bench, a yew-capped hillock on the outskirts of Lyndhurst, was named after the family, probably in 1689, or shortly after, when an earlier Charles Paulet became the 1st Duke and was re-appointed Lord Warden of the New Forest. Then at the request of the 3rd Duke, transport links between Burley Lodge and Lyndhurst were improved by the construction of a purpose-built road which, in part, still shows on modern maps as the Cut Walk.

The Route

1. Leave the car park, turn right and walk along Lyndhurst Road for around 300 metres.

2. Turn right along a gravel cycle track beside Burley New Cottage (by the Burley Products sign), and follow the track straight ahead, initially uphill, into Burley New Inclosure.

    Pass a grassy ride on the left and, as the cycle track bears left, pass another ride on the right. Pass two more rides – one on the right and one on the left – and when 1 kilometre (0.6 miles) from Burley New Cottage, pass an area of fenced clear-fell on the right. Immediately after, go straight ahead at a crossroads – the left turn is another branch of the cycle track. Alongside the route here, on the right, is Cockroad Hill.

3. Continue for around 650 metres, enter Burley Old Inclosure through a gate, and go on downhill beside a low, bracken-covered inclosure boundary bank bordering Dames Slough Inclosure.

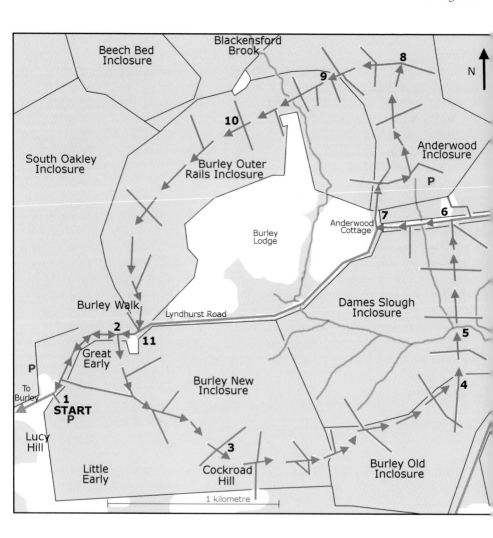

4. After 1 kilometre, follow the track as it goes round to the left, passes through a gap in the inclosure boundary bank, and enters Dames Slough Inclosure.

   Continue downhill, go over a crossroads with gravel track on the left and grassy ride on the right, and proceed across an open landscape relatively recently cleared of whatever tree cover was present.

5. Cross a bridge over a narrow stream and climb a gentle incline before, after around 600 metres, going through a gate and joining a minor road.

6. Turn left along the road and then eventually right, alongside Anderwood Cottage. *The date 1876 and two pairs of deer antlers adorn the walls of this black and white, New Forest keeper's cottage, although for much of the year vegetation obscures both date and antlers.*

   Pass on the left, Anderwood End Cottages, a pair of timber-built sustainable rural homes constructed by the Forestry Commission on the Crown lands to provide rented accommodation for commoners – part of the Forestry Commission's support for the New Forest's historic way of life. The timber frame was made from Douglas firs taken from Anderwood Inclosure; rainwater is collected, filtered and re-used; natural heat from the earth is utilised; and solar energy from the sun is harnessed to produce electricity.

7. Immediately after the cottages, go through a gate into Anderwood Inclosure. Continue straight ahead along a gravel cycle track and, after a short distance, follow the track as it bears right at a junction with two grassy rides. Stay on the cycle track as it next bears left, and immediately pass on the right another track, this one leading up a modest incline. After around 300 metres, go straight ahead, downhill, as the cycle track passes at a crossroads, grassy, overgrown rides to left and right.

8. Turn left at a T-junction – cycle track sign number 16 – and shortly after, pass a grassy ride on the left with here, an indistinct track on the right. After a further 250 metres, pass another grassy ride on the left; immediately after, take the left fork at a Y-junction of gravel cycle tracks; and enter Burley Outer Rails Inclosure.

9. Continue downhill, pass two grassy rides on the left, go straight ahead at a minor crossroads (there are grassy rides to left and right here) and cross a railed bridge over the Blackensford Brook, a typically attractive, gravel-bottomed New Forest stream – to the left here can be seen the grounds of Burley Lodge.

   Continue on up a gentle incline.

10. Go straight ahead at a crossroads where the turn to the right leads along another cycle track. Ignore turns to left and right, and after around 1.5 kilometres (1 mile), go through a gate into a corridor of glorious, ancient, unenclosed woodland. Pass another cycle track on the right, and rejoin Lyndhurst Road.

11. Turn right and return to the car park, which is a short distance away on the left.

For the adventurous, for those with a good sense of direction, strong map reading skills and access to an Ordnance Survey map!
Create your own walk by combining parts of this route with elements of your choice from the following selection of connecting or conveniently located nearby routes.

From *New Forest Walks – a seasonal wildlife guide*:
Walk 10   Barrow Moor, Mark Ash Wood

Walk 14
Burley: Shappen Hill, Burbush Hill, Church Moor, Castle Hill and Honey Lane

Setting the scene

Starting amidst a straggle of ancient, unenclosed woodland, this walk passes over gorse-clad heathlands overlooking an undulating landscape of shallow valleys and somewhat odd-shaped hillocks. Church Moor - the name probably reflects the presence of one of the New Forest's largest Bronze Age barrows, with its similarity of purpose to a graveyard - is on the route, and so is a modest climb up to Castle Hill's aged fort.

After following a wooded ridge-way, the path drops rapidly down towards Honey Lane, an ancient, sunken track used, no doubt, by the smugglers who once operated in these parts. Return towards Burley village and the car park is along Pound Lane, which presumably was the site of the local animal pound.

Commoners' cattle on Church Moor

Start	Burley, Forestry Commission car park, almost opposite the track alongside Burley Primary School on the minor road leading uphill from the Queens Head towards the village cricket pitch, and on to the A35 at Holmsley - Ordnance Survey map reference SU214028
Distance	7 kilometres (4¼ miles)
Time to allow	1¾ - 4¼ hours
Refreshments	The Queens Head and the Burley Inn are both in Burley village
Route	Largely along readily visible tracks, although in places a little 'off the beaten track'
Terrain	Mainly on level ground, but with a small number of quite steep, uphill sections
Rating	2 - moderate walking
Buggies	Not suitable
Railway station	Sway, 9.5 kilometres (6 miles)
Bus service	Wilts and Dorset, primarily on Mondays, Wednesdays and Fridays only
New Forest Tour Bus	Yes
Alternative starts	1) Burley Cricket, Forestry Commission car park, just across the road from Burley car park 2) Public car park beside the Queens Head, close to Burley village centre 3) Burbush Hill, Forestry Commission car park, on the route, beside the minor road leading from Burley to Bransgore at Ordnance Survey map reference SU202018
Forest Holidays Caravan sites and campsites	1) Holmsley, 5.5 kilometres (3½ miles) 2) Setthorns, 7.75 kilometres (4¾ miles)

Along the way

The Bread Stone - charity begins at home

Tucked into the roadside bank close to the Queens Head, the Bread Stone is one of a number of inscribed stones placed around Burley village by Thomas Eyre, one-time house steward and bailiff to the Burley Manor estate. It is marked on one side 'To Lymington Rest and be thankful', on another 'To Lyndhurst', and finally 'PEACE Restored 27th March 1802', which is a reference to the Napoleonic Wars.

Following Eyre's death in 1829, his charity of shoes, clothes and blankets was, by direction of his Will, 'to be distributed annually by the overseers upon the Stone near the Queen's Head...'

The Bread Stone

The Shappen Hill hoard - there's treasure in the gravel

In 1926, in a small gravel pit cut into Shappen Hill, twelve Bronze Age axes were discovered just 45 cm (18 inches) below the surface. Dating from around 1200

A rainbow illuminates the sky near Shappen Hill

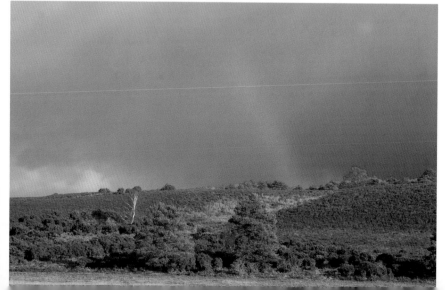

BC, they are now held by the British Museum. All were new and unused, and it has been suggested that they might have been dropped or hidden by a trader en-route to sell goods to people living in and around Castle Hill.

Castleman's Corkscrew – the coming of the railway

The route of an old railway line passes across the heath to the south of Burley. Opened in 1847, it was part of the line running between South-ampton and Dorchester that became known as Castleman's Corkscrew – its main promoter was Charles Castleman, and an eccentrically winding course was chosen to avoid major New Forest woodland areas for fear of accidental fires, and to take-in the already well-established towns of Ringwood and Wimborne.

But in 1888, the Corkscrew was somewhat marginalised when the main London line was extended from Brockenhurst through to Christchurch, which by then already had a rail link to the growing seaside resort of Bournemouth. From 1964, after many years of reducing usage, the old line west of Brockenhurst was progressively closed. A small section of the track-bed alongside Wilverley Inclosure was taken for a new road, but much of the rest in this vicinity remains open for recreation by walkers, cyclists and horse riders.

The remains of Greenberry Bridge

A number of old bridges can still be seen, however, whilst evidence of others can also be found. On the edge of Burbush Hill car park mid-way through this walk, for example, inconspicuous brickwork remains provide a clue to the past, for here, until around 1859, was a short-lived bridge that was demolished to make way for double track operation.

Long Pond – much loved by commoners' stock

Long Pond, a little to the north-west of Burbush Hill, is aptly named, as it is predictably long, and fairly narrow. A moderately shallow, acidic heathland pool, it was mentioned in a Manor Perambulation of 1782 and is also shown and named in the late 18th century on Richardson, King and Driver's map of the area.

Not surprisingly, the pond is a favourite haunt of commoners' ponies, but it is not just the prospect of liquid refreshment that attracts them, for many like nothing better than to wade right in, and feed on the extensive, nourishing growths of waterweed that flourish there.

A pony enjoys a feed in Long Pond

Castle Hill - an Iron Age hillfort

The Bronze Age left barrows aplenty in the New Forest landscape, whilst the succeeding Iron Age bequeathed a small number of earthwork enclosures, such as that at Castle Piece visited during Walk 15, and hillforts similar to the one here at the northern end of the prominent ridge flanking Burley's western approaches.

One of seven hillforts in and around the New Forest, the presence of this relatively small example, which may in part pre-date the Iron Age, seems likely to have had a role in the naming of Burley, for Bur derives from the Anglo-Saxon for a fortification.

A single, in places substantial, bank and the remains of an external silted ditch enclose a broadly oval area of around 2.4 hectares (almost 6 acres). Commanding relatively high ground 90 metres (295 feet) above sea level, defensive potential is immediately apparent. Although parts are now wooded and gravel has been extracted

The relatively high ground of Castle Hill offers obvious defensive potential

from the area within the ramparts, this old place continues to recall ancient tribes and ways of life before the Romans came to Britain. The site offers extensive views to the west and south-west over Vales Moor, Cranes Moor, Kingston Great Common, Strodgemoor Bottom and on over the Avon valley to the hills of Wiltshire and Dorset. Thomas Eyre in 1823 placed nearby an inscribed stone referring to the 'camp or castle', which concluded with the words: 'Be civil, quiet and useful', which even today seems like good advice.

The Route

From the War Memorial Cross in Burley village centre, follow the road signposted to Brockenhurst, Lyndhurst, Lymington and the Church; and pass the Queens Head, a pub with traditional links to local smugglers of old.

Continue along the roadside footpath uphill to the right, past the Bread Stone set into the bank on the left. At the top of the hill, turn right, opposite Burley Primary School (beside signs for Highcroft and the Moorhill House Hotel), along a gravel road.

1. From Burley car park (the Forestry Commission car park across the minor road from the school), leave the car park entrance, turn left along the minor road, and then left again along the gravel road opposite the school.

2. After walking a short distance along the gravel road, take the left fork at the first junction to go downhill towards the Moorhill House Hotel along a narrow tarmac road that in places is an attractive, quite deep hollow-way bordered by moss-clad banks; aged, multi-stemmed hollies; and mature beech and oak trees.

    When close to the bottom of the hill, turn left along a gravel track signposted to Goats Pen Cottage; then when in front of the cottage, pass beside a low, Forestry Commission vehicle barrier and follow the path as, after a short distance, it bears to the right and skirts a copse overlooking open ground away to the left.

3. After a further short distance, ignore a path on the right, close to the trees; and follow the main heathland track up Shappen Hill. Pass turns to left and right close to, and at the top, of the hill; and subsequently ignore other minor paths radiating from the main gravel track that for some considerable distance here runs parallel to the right-hand woodland edge.

4. Eventually, just before a group of birch and holly trees on the right, pass on the right a low, bracken-covered mound that is, in fact, a Bronze Age barrow;

and follow the wide, gravel track as it bears half-left downhill. *To the left here are extensive views over the valley bottom, whilst beyond, at the base of the far hillside, can be seen the prominently embanked route of Castleman's Corkscrew.*

When almost at the bottom of the improbably named Slap Bottom, miss a minor turn on the right and follow the main track as it bears half-left, uphill. Go straight ahead at a hill-top crossroads, pass through a narrow willow and birch corridor, and immediately after, turn right to follow a cycle track along the route of the old railway.

Pass a turn on the right, and where a short length of fencing blocks the way ahead, follow the cycle track to the right, into Burbush Hill car park.

Between the turn passed on the right, and the fence; the route of the old railway intersects a large hummock overgrown with vegetation. Here, to the right of the track, can be glimpsed brickwork of the old bridge separately mentioned.

5. Go through the car park and when halfway along the entrance track, turn half-right. Cross a minor road; ignore a wide, grassy ride running straight ahead close to the edge of a group of conifers; and follow a lesser track half-right over the heath.

6. Pass a little to the right of Long Pond. Again ignore minor paths to left and right, and continue towards a distant straggle of birch, willow and pine trees at Burnt Axon.

    Away to the left here are the extensive heaths and bogs of Cranes Moor, whilst to the right is a ridge of high ground, the site of Burley Beacon and, a little further to the north, Castle Hill.

7. Pass through the line of trees that here borders a rather wet hollow, and cross the narrow stream beyond.

    Notice on a hillock to the left, quite close to the edge of the pines, the Church Moor, Bronze Age barrow that, despite its considerable size, is relatively inconspicuous amongst the bracken.

    Continue straight ahead along an undulating part-sand/part-gravel track, and eventually ignore another pronounced track going uphill on the right at Coffins Holms.

    Coffin was the name of a local family whose Burley roots reach back to the mid-17th century, and maybe earlier.

    To the left of the track here is an unusual hollow-way that opens to a wider valley. The hollow-way does not appear to be man-made, nor does it appear

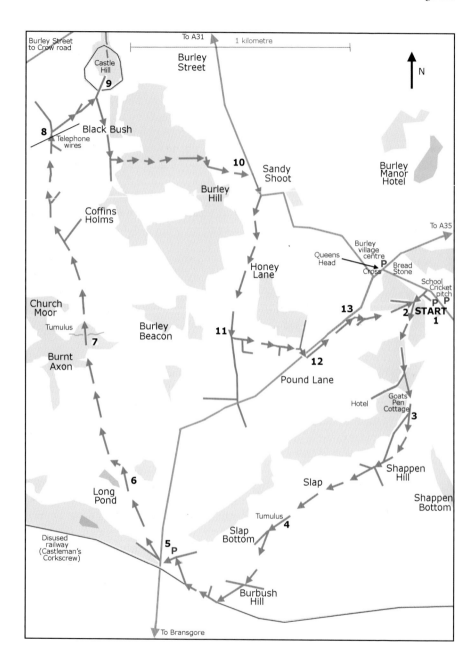

entirely natural. Adjacent to it, at right angles, is a promontory with many conspicuous bumps and hollows that seem to have resulted from use by man, but if so, the time period and purpose are lost in history.

Shortly after, take the left fork at a rather indistinct Y-junction, pass a track on the right and go beneath a line of telephone wires.

8. Immediately after, turn right along a minor track leading up towards Castle Hill, and then when mid-way up, pass a minor track on the left. *The hillside here offers extensive views over the adjacent lowlands, and makes a great place for a refreshment stop.*

   At the top of the hill, turn left along a compacted gravel/dirt track to reach after a short distance the hillfort's single, still impressive earthen bank and external ditch.

9. From the fort, retrace the route and continue along what here is a ridge-way clothed in ancient oaks and beeches. Pass a number of properties to left and right, and eventually, immediately after the driveway for Blackbush Lodge and Blackbush Cottages, go over a stile on the left to follow a meandering public footpath as it goes downhill.

10. At the bottom of the hill, pass through an impressive wrought iron gate beside two bungalows, and turn right along a minor road. After a short distance, as the road bears sharply left, turn right along Honey Lane, an ancient route flanked in its early stages by high, moss-clad banks topped with beech and oak.

    The name Honey Lane has been traced back to 1701, but was probably in use much earlier than this, whilst the trackway is considerably older.

11. Eventually, shortly after a property on the left called Green Pastures and a bungalow on the right called Cherries, go through a gate on the left to follow a narrow footpath that quickly gives way to a wide gravel track, a service road at the rear of a group of houses.

    Immediately pass a road on the right leading into this small estate, and continue along the gravel track. Pass a tarmac road on the right and immediately after, go through a pedestrian gate to continue along Warnes Lane. Ignore here a public footpath on the left.

    The Warne family can be traced back in the village to the early 17th century, whilst the name also recalls that of local 19th century smugglers, Peter and Lovey Warne.

12. Cross a minor road – Pound Lane – and turn left along the adjacent footpath. Pass on the right, the Forest Teahouse and a sign for New Forest Cider; and on the left, Rooks Farm.

    From at least the early 18th century until 1871, the land on which Rooks Farm stands was owned or occupied by successive members of the Rook family, whilst the property is said to date back to 1665.

13. Immediately after Burley Village Hall, turn right along a narrow path leading through an ancient area of diggings that now are of largely natural appearance; and continue uphill, into the woods, for a short distance.

    Meet a gravel track and turn left; reach another junction of tracks – this was passed on the outward route – and retrace your steps back to the walk start point.

For the adventurous, for those with a good sense of direction, strong map reading skills and access to an Ordnance Survey map!
Create your own walk by combining parts of this route with elements of your choice from the following selection of connecting or conveniently located nearby routes.

From *New Forest Walks – a seasonal wildlife guide*:
Walk 12   Burley: Turf Hill, Holmsley Bog

Walk 15
Linwood: Appleslade Inclosure, Rockford Common, Linford Brook, Pinnick Wood and Roe Inclosure

Setting the scene

Not far from the Red Shoot Inn, which makes a convenient refreshment stop, the beginning of this walk is at the south-western end of Linwood. Appleslade Inclosure, woodland dating back to around 1829, is skirted; and so is Rockford Common, an outstanding area of National Trust-owned heathland.

The conifers of Great Linford Inclosure quickly give way to Linford Bottom and the Linford Brook, before Pinnick Wood's ancient landscape is encountered, followed by more intensively managed Roe Inclosure. Ancient woodland is again met with at Amie's Corner and Lin Wood as the walk passes along a short stretch of road leading past the pub and back to the car park.

Roe Cottage stands in a clearing amongst the trees on the edge of Roe Inclosure

Start	Appleslade, Forestry Commission car park, a short distance south-west of Linwood on the road from Emery Down - Ordnance Survey map reference SU185092
Distance	7.25 kilometres (4½ miles)
Time to allow	1¾ - 4½ hours
Refreshments	The Red Shoot Inn is close to the start of the walk
Route	Largely along readily visible tracks, although in and around Pinnick Wood the route is somewhat 'off the beaten track'
Terrain	Mainly on level ground, but with a number of quite steep, uphill sections
Rating	3 - in places, quite strenuous walking
Buggies	Not suitable
Railway station	Ashurst (New Forest), 18 kilometres (11¼ miles)
Bus service	None
New Forest Tour Bus	No
Alternative start	Linford Bottom, Forestry Commission car park at the south-western end of Linford Bottom, 0.5 kilometres (⅓ mile) from the route at Ordnance Survey map reference SU181072 just off the south-western edge of the sketch map.
Forest Holidays Caravan sites and campsites	1) Longbeech, 8.5 kilometres (5¼ miles). 2) Ocknell, 9.5 kilometres (6 miles)

Along the way

Holly - prickly leaved, but with a long history of use by man and beast

Seemingly able to thrive in many of the most shaded places, holly is abundantly present in Pinnick Wood, just as it is elsewhere in the New Forest, even though, despite being armed with prickly leaves, it is intensively browsed by deer and commoners' stock. Indeed, browse lines are often present at the extent of the animals' reach, whilst some heathland hollies have been close-cropped to the strangest of shapes. Yet on open ground, mature hollies

Berry bearing holly branches were commercially cut for use as a Christmas decoration

sometimes occur in roughly circular stands traditionally known as *hats* or *holms*.

Many hollies show evidence of coppicing, their stems periodically cut back to ground level to encourage the repeated growth of new shoots; and pollarding, a similar process executed at a height just out of reach of browsing animals. Such regular cutting can considerably extend tree life, so consequently many New Forest hollies have stool and root systems that probably pre-date by some distance most, if not all, New Forest oaks and beeches.

In days gone by, holly was used extensively as a fodder crop and as raw material for charcoal production. The bark was used from at least the 16th century to make birdlime - a sticky substance used to trap wild birds - whilst the commercial cutting of branches for seasonal decoration was widespread by the early 20th century when, apart from local use, truckloads were taken by rail to London markets.

Today, holly is still cut in winter for the benefit of the stock, whilst pollarding has also recently been resumed so as to prompt re-generation of new wood, and increase the amount of light reaching the woodland floor.

Roe Inclosure - a not-so-logical name

Roe Inclosure has a long history. Trees were first planted in the southern part of the site in around 1700 in what was to become known as Roe Old Inclosure; but in 1811, the earlier planting was subsumed within the fences of a new, considerably extended inclosure. Sadly, the original trees of Roe Old Inclosure have gone, although some of the 1811 oaks remain against a backcloth of more recent conifers and hardwoods.

*The walk route passes through
Roe Inclosure*

But why was the original planting called Roe Inclosure? It's tempting to assume a link with roe deer, but these graceful creatures had probably been hunted to extinction in the New Forest by the end of the 16th century, and did not re-colonise until the second half of the 19th century. Perhaps a few lingered on in this quiet outpost, or maybe Roe was part of a previous name for the site. Possibly roe deer elsewhere provided naming impetus, or Roe may even have been used in error, for in 1609 the area was recorded as Rew End.

Castle Piece - a 'castle' of Iron Age origin

Hidden deep amongst the trees in Roe Inclosure, Castle Piece is a broadly circular enclosure of around 2 hectares (almost 5 acres) surrounded by a large, flattened earthen bank with, in places, an adjacent external ditch. Situated on a modest slope at 61 metres (200 feet) above sea level, the camp, as it is often called, overlooks the Linford Brook and is considered to be of Iron Age origin – the Great Storm of 1987 blew down many oak trees here, which revealed small fragments of probable Iron Age pottery in the root plates.

*Castle Piece: a section of the large,
flattened earthen bank*

The earthwork remains are not as grand as those of many contemporary chalk-land hillforts, nor even as imposing as those associated with the small hillfort at Castle Hill, Burley, but nevertheless, are of significant size. The quite prominent original entrance is a little to the right of the later gap through which the walk route enters the enclosure.

New Forest deer - long may they flourish

Created as a royal hunting ground by William the Conqueror in the late 11th century, the New Forest was, and still is, synonymous with deer. Today four species are regularly seen: fallow, red, roe and sika. Perpetually secretive, muntjac deer introduced from south-east Asia are also present, probably in relatively small numbers, whilst Chinese water deer have also been recorded.

Red deer and roe deer are natives of Britain, although in the New Forest both have experienced periods of difficulty - red deer have survived partly as a result of periodic re-introductions, whilst hunting pressure forced the absence of roe deer for almost 300 years. Red deer numbers are now maintained at up to 180 animals and roe deer at around 400.

Probably introduced by the Normans, fallow deer are abundant and widespread. Numbers are maintained at around 1200 - 1400 animals, a significant reduction from the 9,000 + recorded in the 17th century, but a huge increase on the years following the 1851 Deer Removal Act. Sika deer, meanwhile, were intro-duced from Asia onto the Beaulieu Estate at around the turn of the 19th century, and can now

Roe deer occur in modest numbers

mainly be seen in woodlands south of the railway line and to the east of Brockenhurst. Numbers are main-tained at up to 100 animals.

The Route

1. Go back along the car park approach road and turn left, uphill, alongside the woodland/heathland edge. Reach the corner of Appleslade Inclosure and go half-left onto the open heath, to follow a quite broad track. (A short detour to the right here is worthwhile as it provides good views to the north over Ibsley Common).

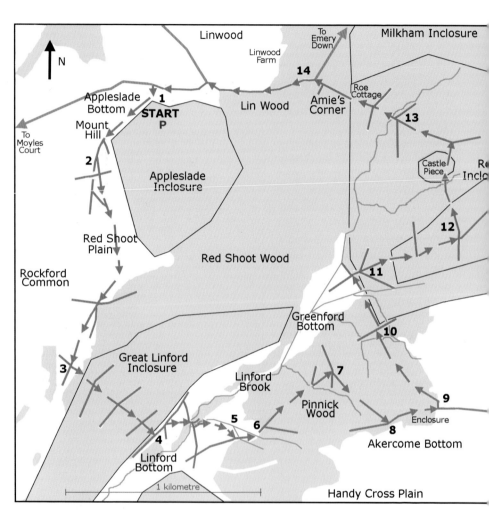

2. Take the next left fork, almost immediately go straight ahead at a crossroads, ignore another track coming in from the right, and follow the main track as it bears half-left.

   Ignore minor pathways to left and right, and continue on towards the edge of Red Shoot Wood. Walk for a short distance beside the wood; go straight ahead at a crossroads; and immediately after, pass a track on the left.

3. Turn left at a relatively indistinct crossroads a little beyond the start of a group of conifers away to the right, and go downhill, initially through a very

narrow strip of ancient, unenclosed woodland; and then immediately through a gate leading into Great Linford Inclosure, a mid-19th century forestry plantation.

Almost immediately, go straight ahead at a crossroads; cross a cycle track and then another crossroads; and leave the inclosure through a gate, this one leading to Linford Bottom, an open area of scattered trees and bracken bordering the Linford Brook.

4. Turn left alongside the inclosure fence; after a short distance, pass a path coming in from the right; and immediately after, turn half-right along another quite narrow path.

   Cross a bridge over the Linford Brook, almost immediately turn right to cross a narrow side-stream at another bridge, and then go left alongside this stream – in places, in summer, it is often dry.

5. Go half-right to follow beside a very narrow drainage channel coming in from the right, or if the ground is particularly wet underfoot, detour further to the right, through the heather.

   Turn left at the edge of Pinnick Wood; cross a drainage channel; continue round, close to the woodland edge; whilst still on the open heath, cross a wider stream with prominent gravel bed; and then follow the quite wide path as it goes into the wood.

6. Almost immediately ignore a narrow path on the right; continue straight ahead for around 400 metres; cross a narrow stream flowing through a pipe below a small, un-railed bridge; and take the main, right fork immediately after the bridge.

7. Turn right at a fairly indistinct junction of tracks close to the top of the hill, ignoring here an at times partly obscured, narrow path leading sharply to the right.

   Continue straight ahead, initially down a gentle gradient, and then up an equally modest gradient. (This part of the route for much of the year can be wet underfoot, so slight detours off the main path may be necessary).

8. Turn left at a T-junction at the edge of the wood – beyond is the open landscape of Akercome Bottom, a small pond, and on the far hilltop, the A31.

   To the right, halfway up this wooded hillside, around 40 metres from the path, is a very low, moss-clad earthen bank enclosing a small oval area. Heywood Sumner, writing in 1917, called it the Fairy Ring Pound, and suggested that it was a 17th century, or earlier, pannage-feeding pig-pound.

9. Briefly emerge from the wood; immediately turn left alongside the woodland edge; and then turn left again, back into the wood, to follow the path downhill. Cross a narrow water channel in the valley bottom, close on the right to the corner of Roe Inclosure.

10. Continue straight ahead for a short distance before turning right at an indistinct T-junction, and then left to follow beside the inclosure wood-bank. *Notice here the stark contrast between the beautiful, haphazardly spaced ancient trees on the left, and the dark serried ranks of inclosure conifers on the right.*

    Step across a narrow water channel and immediately after, cross a bridge over a small, steep-banked stream. After a short distance, turn right, along a cycle track; and go through a gate into Roe Inclosure.

11. Almost immediately go straight ahead at a crossroads; follow the cycle track as it passes through a gap in the bracken-clad wood-bank that once bounded Roe Old Inclosure; and continue to follow the track as, just after, it bears right, uphill. Pass a wide, grassy ride on the left, and then turn left to leave the cycle track at the next crossroads.

12. Continue uphill and eventually out of what was Roe Old Inclosure – there is another break in the wood-bank. After a short distance, at the top of the hill, enter Castle Piece through a gap in the extremely broad surrounding earthen bank, which in summer is largely obscured by bracken.

    Go downhill; leave Castle Piece through another gap in the bank; and after a short distance, turn left at a T-junction to follow a cycle track downhill.

13. Go straight ahead at a crossroads where the cycle track goes right, cross a bridge over the Linford Brook and continue uphill towards white-washed Roe Cottage.

    Go straight ahead at another crossroads, and through a gate beside the cottage to continue for a short distance along a gravel track through ancient, unenclosed woodland.

14. Reach a minor road and turn left. The car park is 1 kilometre (0.6 miles) away.

Walk 16
Frogham: Latchmore Brook, Alderhill Inclosure, Hampton Ridge and part of the Ashley Walk Bombing Range

Setting the scene

With only one significant uphill stretch, this fairly gentle stroll close to the western edge of the New Forest begins near the tiny hamlet of Frogham, and is largely within the area once taken by the Practice Range section of the much larger Second World War, Ashley Walk Bombing Range. The landscape now, though, presents an entirely natural appearance as nature long ago reclaimed its own.

Close to the start of the walk is a small, pink cob cottage, once the home of Juliette de Bairacli Levy, author of 'Wanderers in the New Forest'. Abbots Well is nearby and so is Windmill Hill. The route continues beside Ogden's Farm and for a while follows the Latchmore Brook. Heathland features prominently along the way, and woodland variety is provided by Sloden and Alderhill Inclosures. Hampton Ridge provides notable views in all directions.

Waiting for opening time: a donkey outside the Foresters Arms, Frogham

Start	The car park on Abbotswell Road, close to Abbots Well, 2 kilometres (1¼ miles) from the B3078 Fordingbridge to Brook road - Ordnance Survey map reference SU178129. (Turn off the B3078 on the sharp corner between Godshill and Fordingbridge, and follow the sign for Blissford. Cross a ford, and take the next right turn for Frogham and Hyde. Turn left at the next cross-roads, pass the Foresters Arms on the left, and the car park is 500 metres away, on the right.)
Distance	6 kilometres (3¾ miles)
Time to allow	1½ - 3¾ hours
Refreshments	The Foresters Arms is close to the start of the walk - turn left out of the start car park, and the pub is only a short distance away, on the right
Route	Along readily visible tracks
Terrain	Mainly on level ground, but with one quite steep, uphill section
Rating	2 - moderate walking
Buggies	Except after rain, the route in late spring and summer is usually suitable for sturdy buggies, although there is a narrow drainage channel - without a bridge - to negotiate on the edge of Alderhill Inclosure
Railway station	Ashurst (New Forest), 23 kilometres (14¼ miles)
Bus service	Wilts and Dorset serve nearby Fordingbridge
New Forest Tour Bus	No
Alternative start	Ogdens, Forestry Commission car park, on the route near Ogdens Farm - Ordnance Survey map reference SU182124
Forest Holidays Caravan sites and campsites	1) Longbeech, 12.25 kilometres (7½ miles) 2) Ocknell, 13.25 kilometres (8¼ miles)

Along the way

Abbots Well - a centuries-old source of fresh water

Flanked by wooden railings, Abbots Well lies beside a minor road from where it looks out over gorse, heather and bracken-clad heathlands close to Hampton Ridge. Spring water is present within an open, wooden-framed tub set into the ground; and again within another adjacent tub with hinged cover.

Located on the New Forest boundary, the well was mentioned from 1215 to 1301 in boundary perambulations, when it was listed variously as Abbitewelle, Albitewelle,

Abbots Well

Albythewell, Abbetwell and Alleynewell. By 1670, however, the current name was in use. And the abbot in question? That of Beaulieu Abbey, which held lands at nearby Gorley.

Use of the well surely, though, pre-dates these first documentary references, for the spring waters would no doubt have provided refreshment for earlier travellers along Hampton Ridge. Health-giving and curative properties have been ascribed to the waters, although few today are tempted to partake.

Latchmore Shade - respite and rest for the ponies

Adjacent to the Latchmore Brook, Latchmore Shade is one of a number of similarly named places in the New Forest associated with traditional use by sometimes quite large, late spring and summer gatherings of commoners' ponies, present not so much to seek shelter from the sun, but more to avoid the attentions of biting insects.

The ponies are said to *shade*, and their favoured haunts have become known as *shades*. Somewhat contradictorily, however, many New Forest shades are out in the open, exposed to the full glare of the sun, although often in places that experience cooling air currents, and more importantly, where flies are relatively absent.

Of course, a great many unnamed shades exist, and new shades are sometimes adopted, but some, such as that at Latchmore, are of sufficient age to be shown on Ordnance Survey maps. Indeed, others – Markway Shade, close to what is now the A35, and Withycombe Shade, beside the Beaulieu River, are examples – were so named from at least the late 18th century.

A large gathering of commoners' ponies adjacent to the Latchmore Brook

At that time, Latchmore's extensive grasslands were known as Latchmore Green, and they remain a favourite year-round haunt of stock attracted, in part, by the availability of relatively rich grazing and fresh water. Heywood Sumner, writing in 1923, caught well the atmosphere when he described autumn fern carts labouring along deep, rutted tracks; and remarked that 'times changes have left Latchmore untouched'.

Forestry Inclosures – a changing landscape

The view from the incline leading up to Hampton Ridge during Section 8 of this walk brings into sharp relief the 19th century landscape changes that followed the creation of often coniferous, forestry inclosures. Alderhill Inclosure (1864) and Sloden Inclosure (also, largely, 1864) can be seen to the south-east. Holly Hatch (1808) and Broomy (1809) are beyond, whilst on the far horizon are the stark

The edge of Sloden Inclosure to the right, and Alderhill Inclosure to the left

outlines of Milkham (1861) and Slufters (1862). Amberwood (1815) is to the east; and Hasley (around 1846) to the south.

Imagine the hustle and bustle that unfolded here soon after the 1808 and 1851 Acts of Parliament that authorised these inclosures, and the old places that soon were to be engulfed in trees: Long String Bushes, Amberwood Green and Bruin's Bushes, for example, all alongside the now wooded sections of the Latchmore Brook.

It is not surprising, then, that local people so objected to this perceived theft of the old, open Forest where commoners' stock could freely roam, stock that would be excluded from the developing woods until the trees were safe from browsing.

Romano-British potteries - manufacturing industry in the heart of the New Forest

Between the 3rd and early 5th centuries – during the later years of Roman occupation – the New Forest was the site of a commercial pottery industry. Local clay was no doubt pressed into service, fuel to fire the kilns was abundantly available in the old woods, and sandstone used in kiln construction was also to be found nearby.

Kiln sites and pottery fragments of this era have been discovered in Sloden, Pitts Wood, Alderhill, Amberwood and Islands Thorns Inclosures, and in a small number of places elsewhere. Excavation has often been hampered, though, by the wooded nature of the terrain, but an overall picture of activity has, nevertheless, been pieced together.

Initial discoveries were, however, often accidental, as illustrated in the early 1860s by John Wise who remarked: 'From time to time the labourer, in draining

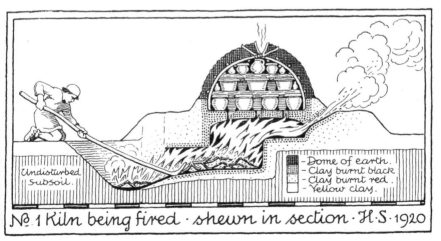

Heywood Sumner's 1920 portrayal of a Romano-British pottery kiln

or planting in the Forest, digs down upon pieces of earthenware, whilst in the turfy spots the mole throws up black fragments in her mound of earth.' Similarly, Heywood Sumner 60 years, or so, later, attributed the accidental detection of a site to the burial of a keeper's pony, and another to the work of rabbits that, in excavating their burrows, threw up black earth and pieces of pottery.

Even now, deep in the woods, pottery fragments can still be found, but gone are the days of the 1960s when much archaeological damage was caused by weekend collecting parties travelling in by car. Today, thankfully, many of these sites are protected by law as Scheduled Ancient Monuments.

Hampton Ridge – travellers' joy along the New Forest spine
Running from the New Forest's western boundary at Abbots Well, north-east to Bramshaw Telegraph, the spine of Hampton Ridge for much of its early course provides impressive views over rugged landscapes of open, undulating heath and bog.

Extensive views can be enjoyed from Hampton Ridge

Bronze Age men sited their barrows along this ancient ridge-way route, and walked the high ground, well above the surrounding, probably impassable, valley bottoms; whilst the Romano-British potters, too, no doubt travelled this way. Isaac Taylor, mid-18th century mapmaker, showed at least part of the route as Southampton Ridge, suggesting use by city-bound travellers. Later in the 18th century, Richardson, King and Driver's map simply had Hampton Ridge, and also associated this name with the ridge to the north now used by the modern road, the B3078; a convention that continued until at least the mid-19th century.

At times, the ridge can be wild and windswept, but it remains a favourite haunt of walkers, cyclists and horse riders, who keep company with deer, commoners' stock and a wide range of birds and other wildlife.

Ashley Walk Bombing Range - the practice range

Now largely forgotten in the south-west corner of the Ashley Walk Bombing Range, the 1,830 metres (6,000 feet) diameter practice range, although relatively little used, was intermittently showered with inert devices and smoke bombs dropped from heights of up to 4267 metres (14,000 feet) during daytime and night-time flights.

The 80 feet long concrete arrow

However, in contrast to the high explosive range visited during Walk 1, little substantial evidence of war-time activity has, until recently, been readily visible, apart from on the site of a high level illuminated target where a number of quite large, concrete light boxes still circle the target area.

But, whilst a low level practice target – a simple chalk triangle – remains largely obscured by vegetation; high on Hampton Ridge, a 24 metres (80 feet) long concrete arrow pointing towards the illuminated target has recently been rescued from a similar fate following cleaning and scrub removal. Similarly rejuvenated, nearby concrete slabs – originally with lights – and a 14 metres (46 feet) x 7.5 metres (24½ feet) compass, marked out in chalk, would have provided further navigational assistance. Adjacent evidence of a building may signify the location used for plotting target practice results, and to house the diesel-engined generator that powered both the 'concrete slab' lights and the illuminated target lights.

Thompson's Castle - another mystery

Thompson's Castle, a series of heathery, connected hillocks circled round in horseshoe shape, can be

A broad, well-worn track leads over Thompson's Castle

found in the valley bottom to the south of Hampton Ridge. The name has been in use since at least the 18th century, although there is no evidence to suggest that a conventional castle was ever present here.

Elsewhere in the New Forest, however, Castle Hill, Burley, is the site of an ancient hillfort; whilst Castle Piece, deep in Roe Inclosure, surrounded by a substantial earthen bank, is considered to be an Iron Age camp. But there are no such banks at Thompson's Castle; nor, except for a number of small, overgrown diggings, are there any other earthworks. So who was Thompson, and why was this known as his castle? Maybe we will never know.

Volunteer Rifle Range - home of Colonel Vandeleur's sharp shooters

Close to Long Bottom, just below Hampton Ridge, a marker's hut set into the hillside and a nearby target structure - a favourite sheltering place for commoners' ponies - are reminders of a Volunteer rifle range established in 1894 under the direction of Colonel Vandeleur of the 4th Battalion Hants Rifle Volunteer Corps. For much of the year engulfed in vegetation, the marker's hut is no doubt original, but the target structure, which still retains parts of the original mechanisms, would appear to be of later date.

The firing position, close to Blissford, was 732 metres (800 yards) to the west. The 1909 Ordnance Survey map shows the marker's hut and targets; whilst in 1898, a magazine a little to the south-west of the marker's hut is also named. The presence of a range was also indicated on a 1943 New Forest Training Areas map, which might explain the apparently later origin of the target structure.

The rifle range marker's hut

The Route

1. Leave the car park at its main entrance and turn right, down the minor road. Pass on the right Abbots Well; and as the road goes sharply left, turn right along a rutted, gravel track beside Windmill Hill, an exposed site that was possibly suitable for the location of a windmill, although evidence of this use is lacking. (Vehicle access is prohibited here, but walkers may pass through).

2. Continue downhill; pass Ogden's Farm on the right; go beside a low, Forestry Commission vehicle barrier; and cross a small bridge over the Latchmore Brook.

3. Turn left through Ogdens car park, and continue straight ahead, parallel to the course of the brook, alongside a wide expanse of natural stream-side lawn.

4. At the end of the lawn, turn right and then almost immediately left along a wide, grassy ride beside a series of low mounds similar to those found on Balmer Lawn, Brockenhurst.

   To the right here are a series of heather-clad hillocks that include Great Witch and Little Witch, names that, with Witch spelt as Wytch, date back to at least the 18th century. Richardson, King and Driver's map, though, somewhat confusingly shows Great Wytch as Little Wytch, and Little Wytch as Great Wytch! But was witchcraft ever undertaken here, or were these hillocks named after a fancied similarity to witches' hats? Maybe one or the other, although a derivation associated with the Old English word wisc, meaning marshland, has also been suggested.

   Also nearby are the remains of the Ashley Walk Bombing Range high level illuminated target and low level practice target. Beware, though, if diverting from the main route to find the high level illuminated target, for even in summer the ground can be very wet.

5. When quite close to the edge of Alderhill Inclosure, follow a well-worn track between the damp, stream-side ground on the left, and the mature heather on the right. Step across a narrow side-stream at the edge of the inclosure, and continue straight ahead alongside the inclosure fence.

6. After a short distance, ignore a track going half-right across the heath beside Sloden Inclosure, and immediately pass a gate on the left – a turn through this

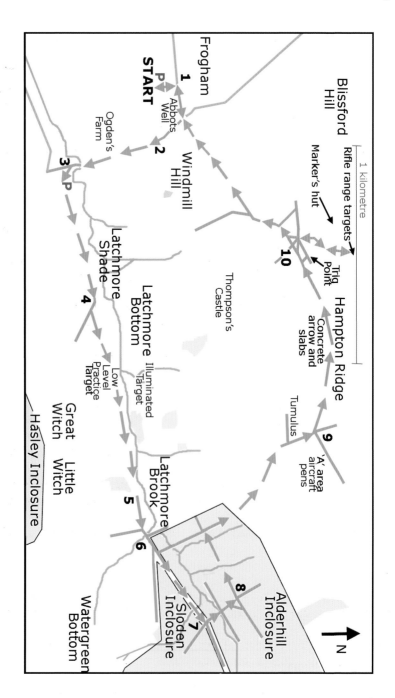

gate provides a shortcut, but the path is intersected by the Latchmore Brook which at many times of year cannot easily be crossed.

Continue along a wide, grassy ride between the conifers of Sloden Inclosure on the right, and Alderhill Inclosure on the left; and past a gate on the right where the Sloden conifers give way to oaks remaining from the original planting.

7. Reach a small stock pound on the right, and turn left along an adjacent gravel track to enter Alderhill Inclosure through a gate.

   Cross a bridge over the Latchmore Brook; go straight ahead where a grassy ride intersects the gravel track; and then where the gravel track bears right, continue straight on, up a slight incline where on the left can be found a sturdy wooden seat, an ideal place for a coffee stop: quiet, secluded, beside the stream – what more could be asked?

   A plaque informs that the seat was placed here: 'In memory of Eric Ashby MBE, 1918 to 2003, Naturalist, pioneer wildlife film maker and President of the New Forest Badger Group'.

8. After a short distance, turn left along another gravel track, here flanked on both sides by conifers. Follow the track to the right at the next crossroads, leave the inclosure through a gate, and follow the track half-left, uphill, to Hampton Ridge.

   The inconspicuous low mound of a Bronze Age barrow lies to the left of this track; whilst to the right, just outside the Practice Range boundary, is the site of aircraft dispersal pens.

9. At the top of the hill, turn left to follow the spine of the ridge along a substantial gravel cycle track.

   The Practice Range concrete arrow, slabs and compass are visible on the left along here – towards the western end of the second, quite substantial promontory.

   Ignore minor tracks to left and right, and eventually pass a trig point a little distance away to the right.

To view the site of the 19th century volunteer rifle range:

Immediately after the trig point, and just before a crossroads where the left-hand turn runs downhill towards Thompson's Castle; turn right, along a gravel track leading slightly uphill.

Continue for a short distance, reach a six-way junction of tracks, take the track on the right going off at around 90 degrees, and follow this as, after a short distance, it bears round a little to the right and continues downhill.

The marker's hut is tucked into the lower reaches of the hillside on the left, whilst the target structure is on the right, beside the track and adjacent to another hill.

10. Otherwise, continue along the main gravelled cycle track leading back to Abbots Well, and from there retrace your footsteps back to the car park.

For the adventurous, for those with a good sense of direction, strong map reading skills and access to an Ordnance Survey map!
Create your own walk by combining parts of this route with elements of your choice from the following selection of connecting or conveniently located nearby routes.

From *New Forest Walks – a time traveller's guide*:
Walk 1   Ashley Walk Bombing Range
Walk 2   Bramshaw Telegraph

From *New Forest Walks – a seasonal wildlife guide*:
Walk 1   Godshill Cricket

Glossary

Agister – employees of the Verderers, responsible for a range of duties mostly associated with the welfare of the commoners' stock.

Ancient and Ornamental woodlands – old, semi-natural, unenclosed, pasture woodlands.

Bailiwick – an administrative area of the Forest. There were nine of them, of which Burley Bailiwick was the largest – this existed from at least the 13th century to the early 19th century.

Bottom – as in a valley bottom.

Broadleaved trees – oak, ash, beech and others with broad-bladed leaves, as opposed to the narrow, needle-shaped leaves of conifers.

Browse – leaves, young shoots and twigs of trees and shrubs on which animals feed.

Browse line – a horizontal skirt on hollies and other trees, at the extent of reach of browsing deer and commoners' animals.

Browsing – the action of animals when feeding on leaves, young shoots and twigs of trees or shrubs.

Clear-fell – the complete, or almost complete, removal of trees by felling. Sometimes clear-felled areas are left to regenerate naturally, sometimes they are re-planted.

Commoner – one entitled to make use of common rights.

Commoning – the use of common rights.

Common rights – entitlements associated with land or property that allow use of Forest land and resources. The rights of fuelwood, mast and pasture continue to be regularly exercised; whilst common of pasture for sheep is much less used. The rights of marl and turbary are no longer in use.

Coppiced trees – trees, such as hazel and holly, cut off at ground level to encourage the growth of new shoots.

Disafforest – remove from an area, the legal status of Forest.

Dispark – to throw open a park.

Drift – the late summer/autumnal round-up, mainly of ponies, that enables the animals to be, for example, checked over, wormed and tail marked to signify payment of the annual marking fee.

Driftway – a corridor of open land left between blocks of woodland for the convenience of those undertaking drifts.

Estovers – an alternative name for Common of Fuelwood.

Forest – a legally designated area that was subject to Forest Law.

Grazing – the action of animals when feeding on grass and other ground level vegetation.

Groomkeeper – a keeper responsible for undertaking day-to-day duties within a walk.

Gutter – a small stream.

Hat – a relatively small, roughly circular area of woodland, often on open ground, and usually with mature hollies conspicuously present.

Hollow-way – a sunken path or trackway.

Holm – see hat.

Inclosure – woodland created using the provisions of the New Forest Acts of 1698, 1808, 1851 or 1949.

Incroachment – Forest land occupied illegally.

Lord Warden – until 1850, the Lord Warden was virtually the Forest's most senior officer.

Marking fee – the annual fee paid by commoners for each animal depastured on the Forest.

Master keeper – a person appointed by the Lord Warden, with bailiwick-wide responsibilities.

Pannage season – the period when pigs are put out on the Forest to fatten on acorns and beech mast.

Pasture woodlands – unenclosed woodlands frequented by deer and commoners' animals.

Perambulation – the legal boundary of the Forest.

Pollard – a tree cut off at a little above head height to encourage new growth out of reach of deer and commoners' animals.

Purlieu – land once within the jurisdiction of the Forest, but no longer so.

Re-seeded lawn – an area re-seeded in the mid-20th century, often after arable cropping, to increase the pasturage available to commoners' animals.

Ride – a relatively wide pathway through woodland.

Shade – a traditionally used area frequented by commoners' animals, particularly ponies, in late spring and summer.

Statutory Inclosure – woodland created using the provisions of the New Forest Acts of 1698, 1808 or 1851.

Tail marking – the cutting of hair on ponies' tails to denote that the related annual marking fee has been paid. The shape of the cut denotes the Agister's area that the pony most often frequents.

Thrown out – the removal of fences placed around an inclosure to prevent access by deer and commoners' animals. Undertaken when the trees are sufficiently well-grown to withstand browsing pressure.

Turves – units of peaty turf once dug for fuel by those entitled so to do - those to whom common of turbary applied.

Underkeeper – see groomkeeper.

Unenclosed woodlands – old, semi-natural woodlands - sometimes known as Ancient and Ornamental woodlands and pasture woodlands - that are unfenced and therefore commonly frequented by deer and commoners' animals.

Verderer – a member of the Verderers' Court.

Verderers' Court – originally a judicial body dating back to at least the 13th century, the court now works to protect, administer, conserve and safeguard New Forest commoning practices and traditional landscapes, wildlife and aesthetic character.

Verderers' Inclosures – inclosures created with the agreement of the Verderers using the provisions of the New Forest Act, 1949. The Act empowered the Verderers to authorise the Forestry Commission to enclose up to a further 2,025 hectares (5,000 acres) of open land for plantations, upon payment of compensation. Additionally, broad, re-seeded grazing strips were also offered around the edge of the new inclosures. Dibden Inclosure, Fawley Inclosure and Ipley Inclosure are all examples from the eastern section of the Forest. None of these are encountered during these walks.

Walk – the unit of land for which a groomkeeper/underkeeper was responsible. The area within each walk originally corresponded to that of a bailiwick, but some bailiwicks later contained multiple walks.

Water – as in, for example, Highland Water. A reasonably substantial stream.

Acknowledgements

An enormous debt of gratitude is due to many past chroniclers of the New Forest whose material has been available for reference. In particular, mention must be made of the mid-19th century work of John R. Wise; of Heywood Sumner in the early 20th century; and more recently, Colin R. Tubbs; Anthony Pasmore; members of the Hampshire Field Club and Archaeological Society, New Forest Section; and members of the New Forest History and Archaeology Group.

Special thanks are also due to Richard Reeves, Librarian at The Christopher Tower New Forest Reference Library, Lyndhurst, who kindly provided much invaluable assistance, reference material, and new and updated information based on his own painstaking research and publications. Richard helped unravel numerous contradictions in previously published works, and also commented on an early draft version of this book.

Alan Brown, author of *They Flew from the Forest* and *Twelve Airfields*, provided information about New Forest airfields and also commented on a draft of the walk around Beaulieu Heath's Second World War airfield. Norman Parker, co-author of *Ashley Walk: its Bombing Range, Landscape and History*, patiently and helpfully answered my questions about the site, and commented on a draft of the related walk. Sue Westwood, Clerk to the New Forest Verderers, provided useful general information; and so did Richard Daponte, Forest Ranger with the Forestry Commission.

And finally, I would like to thank a number of friends who checked the walk instructions and provided extremely helpful comments. Thanks, then, go to Geoff, Mairi and Richard Aston, Steve and Margaret Boswell, Linda Bradshaw, Madalaine Cintra, John and Eileen Howell, Sue O'Brien, Kåre and Lisbet Olerud, Peter and Pat Smith, Mark Winnington, Karen Davies and Paul Worley.

Needless-to-say, however, any errors or omissions are entirely my own responsibility.

References

Books

A Guide to the New Forest – Heywood Sumner

A Wild Heritage: The History and Nature of the New Forest – Terry Heathcote

Ancient Trackways of Wessex – H.W. Timperley and Edith Brill

Ashley Walk: its Bombing Range, Landscape and History – Anthony Pasmore and Norman Parker

Before We Go: Brockenhurst Memories of Peace and War – Compiled by Richard Taylor

Birds of Hampshire – Hampshire Ornithological Society

Castleman's Corkscrew: The Southampton and Dorchester Railway 1844-1848 – J.G. Cox

Comyn's New Forest: 1817 directory of life in the parishes of Boldre & Brockenhurst – Henry Comyn

Discovering the New Forest – Terry Heathcote

Domesday Book, Hampshire – General Editor, John Morris

Handbook of the Birds of Europe, the Middle East and North Africa – The Birds of the Western Palearctic – Stanley Cramp et al

Heywood Sumner's Wessex – selected and introduced by Barry Cunliffe

Historical Atlas of Breeding Birds in Britain and Ireland, 1875-1900 – Simon Holloway

History of British Mammals – Derek Yalden

Lyndhurst: A Brief History and Guide – Georgina Babey and Peter Roberts

Minstead: Life in a 17th Century New Forest Community – Peter Roberts

New Forest Explosives: An Account of the Schultze Gunpowder Company of Eyeworth and the Armaments Research Department, Millersford – Edited by Anthony Pasmore

New Forest Ponies – Valerie Russell

New Forest Pottery Kilns and Earthworks – Anthony Pasmore

New Forest Roe Deer – John K. Fawcett

New Forest Walks – Peter Evening

Papers produced for Lyndhurst Historical Society by Roy Jackman, B.E.M.

Proceedings of the Hampshire Field Club and Archaeological Society, 1938, Volume 14: Hampshire Barrows – L.V. Grinsell

Proceedings of the Hampshire Field Club and Archaeological Society, Volumes 45, 46 and 48: Silvicultural Inclosure in the New Forest to 1977 – David Stagg

Proceedings of the Hampshire Field Club and Archaeological Society, Volume 54: The Earthwork Remains of Enclosure in the New Forest – Nicola Smith
Proceedings of the Hampshire Field Club and Archaeological Society, Volume 54: Ancient New Forest trees – Chris Read
Rambles by Rail – Malcolm S. Trigg
Records of Burley – Miss F. Hardcastle, B.E.M.
The New Forest: its History and its Scenery – John R. Wise
The New Forest – C.J. Cornish
The New Forest: An Ecological History – Colin R. Tubbs
The New Forest: A Natural History – Colin R. Tubbs
The New Forest at War – John Leete
They Flew from the Forest – Alan Brown
Thirty-Five Years in the New Forest – Gerald Lascelles
Traditional Charcoal Making in the New Forest – Richard Reeves
Turnpike Trust Roads in the Lyndhurst Area – Alan Brown
Twelve Airfields – Alan Brown

Maps

Isaac Taylor's Map of Hampshire and the Isle of Wight, 1759
Richardson, King, Driver and Driver's New Forest map, 2nd Edition, 1814 – Courtesy of the New Forest Association
Ordnance Survey maps, 1870, 1898 and 1909 – Courtesy of the Hampshire Record Office

Web resources

English Monarchs – www.englishmonarchs.co.uk
New Forest District Deer Management Plan – www.forestry.gov.uk/pdf/new-forest-deer-plan-2005-2015.pdf/$FILE/new-forest-deer-plan-2005-2015.pdf
New Forest Inclosures – www.forestry.gov.uk
New Forest Notes by Anthony Pasmore - the draining of Balmer Lawn – www.geodata.soton.ac.uk
New Forest Union Workhouse – www.workhouses.org.uk
World War I Trench Dogs – www.roll-of-honour.com
Turnpike roads – www.turnpikes.org.uk

Index

Also from Sigma Leisure:

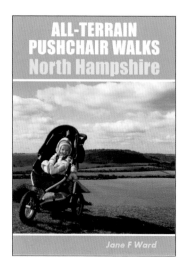

All-Terrain Pushchair Walks
North Hampshire
Jane F Ward

30 carefully selected all-terrain buggy walks in beautiful North Hampshire. From strolls through ancient forests, heathland rambles to spectacular uplands romps. Whether you're walking to keep fit or to enjoy the great outdoors, this book features detailed walk descriptions together with clear maps, local attractions and where to get refreshments.
£8.99

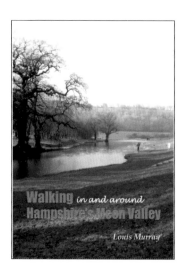

Walking in and around Hampshire's Meon Valley
Louis Murray

The river Meon is one of Hampshire's quintessential chalk streams. It rises from natural springs in the South Downs to the south of the village of East Meon. This book contains the details of 20 walks in the Meon river valley area in southern Hampshire. The walks are suitable for novices, casual walkers, family groups, and experienced ramblers.
£8.99